# Life to the Full

Essentials for Following Jesus

Steven Anderson

James Renwick

Published by Healing Rooms Scotland, PO Box 7010, Glasgow G76 0WF United Kingdom. Telephone 0044 (0)141 637 4445
www.healingrooms-scotland.com

Printed in the United Kingdom ISBN 978-0-9562397-2-3

# Introduction

## *Life to the Full*

Many advertisements make all sorts of claims about how their product will give us a better, more fulfilled, happier life. Not all of them deliver what they promise and not many stand the test of time. Jesus made an amazing claim too. He said that he had come to give us life in all its fullness. Some 2,000 years on, Jesus' claim still seems to work according to the testimony of vast numbers of people throughout the world.

**So what is it that makes the life he offers so fulfilling?**
First he invites and challenges us to an adventure of following him, doing the things he did and living in a whole new way with new values. Second he introduces us to God the Father, and launches us on a life-long exploration of getting to know the heart of God. Third he brings a whole new dimension into our lives through the Holy Spirit that makes possible a true transformation of our lives, enabling and empowering us to become all that God ever intended for us to be.

We are drawn into a whole new set of relationships – with God, with other people and even in how we relate to ourselves. Life is largely about relationships as the theme of many a song and film will tell us. It is in relationship that we get our sense of identity – of who we are; a sense of security or indeed insecurity; and a sense of significance, or not, about our lives. As we come into relationship with God we gain a new sense of identity, security and true significance about our lives, no longer based on our achievements, and affected by our failures, but based on God's incredible love and acceptance of us as his children.

We are no longer controlled by our past, but as forgiven and free people we walk, and sometimes run, into this new life that opens up to us the endless possibilities of a relationship with the eternal God.

As you walk through the pages of this manual may you discover the wonderful riches that Jesus Christ has for you, and may you embark on this great adventure with him to bring the influence of his love, peace and power to your world.

**How to use this manual**
Our heart for this manual is not just to bring about information but also transformation. Therefore each section holds a variety of ways to explore the topic and more importantly, has keys to help you build each of them into your own life as you start or continue this incredible journey. We don't want to just know these things in our heads but we need to be able to relate to them and live them out, as that is where the real benefit and the power comes. Living life to the full is not supposed to be just a theory.

Each section takes on the same format:
*Teaching:* A short teaching on the topic with some thoughts from the writers.
*Illustration:* This may take the form of someone's own personal story, one from the writers' experience or maybe an illustration to

make the topic even more "real."

*Have a look:* Allows you to explore for yourself what the Word of God says.

*Practical Response:* Rather than just read about it, let's do something about it!

*Questions:* Time of reflection to really ask yourself:  What does this mean to me?

*Growth Point:* An idea that will help even further in the understanding of the topic and for putting it in place for your journey.

This manual can be used on an individual basis. However it could also be helpful to go through it with others who are at the early stages of their walk with God, or with someone you trust that could help you with questions and can be there to explore things further with you.

We believe that a key part of making the most of this manual is for you to decide what you will put into it. We live in such a consumerist society; we are so used to being the audience, but God calls us to get involved. Rather than just watching a movie or being a sports spectator, God says: Come and be part of it. It is much more exciting! Therefore we encourage you to take the time, in each section, for it to go deep within your heart and your mind, so that each of these things becomes part of your day-to-day living and you will really experience this life to the full as promised by Jesus.

# Part 1 – This is your God

## *Introduction*

---

*Josh had often been misunderstood and judged by those who had heard rumours and half-truths about him. Some had perceived that he was a harsh man; others had heard he was distant and far-removed from people. Still others thought of him as a killjoy, out to spoil everyone's fun. Some had heard marvellous stories of some of his exploits from long ago and wondered if these accounts were actually true. Others however believed these to be mere myths and exaggerations. However, those who actually knew him would say that if you got to know him you would be wonderfully surprised to find out what he really is like.*

---

In this opening section we will look at who Jesus is and what he did that was so important; the God he introduces us to as Father, and the slightly mysterious sounding Holy Spirit whom Jesus imparts to those who believe in him. These three Persons – Father, Son and Holy Spirit – comprise what we call the Trinity; One God who expresses himself in three Persons.

As the Christian life is rooted in and flows from our relationship with God, it is most important that we get to know, understand and experience him as he reveals himself to us. The Apostle Paul sums this up in his closing words in a letter he wrote to one of the churches: "*The amazing grace of Jesus Christ (the Son), the*

---

*extravagant love of God (the Father), the intimate friendship of the Holy Spirit, be with all of you"* (2 Corinthians 13:14, The Message Bible).

# 1. Who is Jesus?

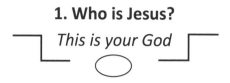

*This is your God*

*"...Jesus asked, 'Who do you say I am?' Peter answered, 'you are the Christ, the Son of the Living God'..."*

That's a really important question: who do you say Jesus is? Jesus thought that Peter gave a really good answer, not because he was especially smart, but because this was revealed to him from God. Faith in Jesus starts with a revelation that leads you into a relationship.

**What else does the Bible reveal to us about who Jesus was and is?**
The Bible gives many names and descriptions of Jesus. During his life on earth he was known as Jesus of Nazareth as that was simply where he had grown up. He referred to himself often as the Son of Man, and his followers began to recognise that he was the Son of God. The New Testament gives many other names that reveal more of Jesus' character, nature and activity – the Light of the world, the Lamb of God, the Good Shepherd, the Resurrection and the Life, the First and the Last, and many more. Part of our journey of getting to know him comes through exploring these many names and their significance.

The church over the centuries has recognised that Jesus is the Son of God, who came to earth, born of the Virgin Mary through the power of the Holy Spirit, who lived as a man and was fully human.

He is also recognised to be fully God, who laid aside his glory and came to die for the sin of humankind. This is all very significant in terms of what he has accomplished on our behalf and how we can relate to him.

As a man he experienced what we experience – tiredness, hunger, emotions and so forth, so we know that he can understand our struggles. As the Son of God he is the only one able to truly mediate between God and humankind. Jesus is the true representation of God – he shows us in human form what God is truly like. If our 'picture' of God doesn't fit with what Jesus was like, then there is something faulty with that picture.

Through the whole Bible story from beginning to end, Jesus is the central character; his coming was foretold hundreds of years before he was born. He is the hero who comes on the scene to liberate us from all that would destroy life. He is the one through whom we interpret the whole story.

**'Christ and Saviour.'**
Two very important names given to Jesus are Christ and Saviour. 'Jesus Christ' - so often misused as swear words – means Jesus the Anointed One, that is, the One who is endowed with God's Spirit for a special purpose. That special purpose is summed up in the name 'Saviour.' In the narrative around Jesus' birth, the angel announces to Joseph that he is to give this child the name 'Jesus' as 'he will save his people from their sins' (Matthew 1:21). Jesus (like the name Joshua in the Old Testament) means 'the Lord saves' or the idea of

'God to the rescue.' Matthew's Gospel goes on to show that Jesus' birth was a fulfilment of the prophecy of Isaiah that "the virgin will give birth to a son, and they will call him 'Immanuel' – which means 'God with us'" (Matthew 1:23).

All this could be summed up by saying that Jesus was God's Son, the special envoy sent from heaven, who in fact is God himself (God with us), who came to rescue and save us. In the next chapter we will look at what he saved us from and for, and how he did that.

The first Christians in the New Testament summed up their faith in three simple words – 'Jesus is Lord!' That was the expression of their belief and experience that Jesus had conquered all of his and our enemies, especially the final enemy of death. He is risen from the dead, and those first disciples were witnesses of this as he appeared to them on several occasions, so they declared with confidence that he was Lord of all.

*"Over the years of getting to know Jesus I have found him to be true to what he said. He is like the very best friend who is always there – supportive, faithful, totally trustworthy and honest enough to confront my mistakes. He is not controlling but releasing; he doesn't condemn but forgives; he doesn't wound but heals. He is undoubtedly the man I admire the most. I am more impressed with him and what he did and does than with anyone else. As I remain impressed with him, he makes his impression on me, and so day by day I trust that I am becoming more like him."*

**Have a look**

Look up the following verses in John's Gospel in the Bible and write down how Jesus described himself, and then write what that term means to you.

John 8:12 "I am ........................................................................"

...........................................................................................

...........................................................................................

...........................................................................................

John 10:14 "I am ....................................................................."

...........................................................................................

...........................................................................................

...........................................................................................

John 11:25 "I am ....................................................................."

...........................................................................................

...........................................................................................

...........................................................................................

**Practical Response: Develop the Relationship**

Jesus called a very ordinary group of guys to be his followers (disciples) – to hang out with him, talk with him, watch him and do what he did. Take some time this week to 'be with Jesus' – to think about who he is, to chat to him about your life, and to listen and watch for how he might want to communicate with you.

**Questions for Reflection:**

1. Do you believe Jesus understands what you go through in life, and that he can help you in meaningful ways?

2. What did or do you need Jesus to rescue you from?

3. What might 'following Jesus' look like in your life?

**\*\*\*\*\*\*\*\*\***

### Growth Point:

Get a modern translation of the Bible if you don't already have one, such as the New International Version or the New Living Translation. You can see various translations on websites like www.biblegateway.com or can use an online Bible like www.youversion.com. Read John's Gospel chapter 1 and find out more about who Jesus is.

**\*\*\*\*\*\*\*\*\***

## 2. What did Jesus do?

*This is your God*

*"For what I received I passed on to you as of first importance: that Christ died for our sins according to the Scriptures, that he was buried, that he was raised on the third day"*
*- Paul the Apostle*

Jesus was born in Bethlehem probably around 6 BC (the original working out of BC and AD was slightly out) and grew up in a town called Nazareth in northern Israel. As he grew he became increasingly aware of who he really was and the purpose of his life, but he didn't appear in a public manner until he was around 30 years of age. At that time John the Baptist, who was the first prophet to appear in Israel for some 400 years, came on the scene calling people to turn back to God, and as a sign of this to be baptised in water in the River Jordan. Jesus himself was baptised, though he had no need to be, as he had lived a sinless life. At this baptism, the heavens opened to him, he was filled with the Holy Spirit, and heard a voice from heaven saying "This is my Son, whom I love; with him I am well pleased" (Matthew 3:17).

Now Jesus launched on his public ministry, proclaiming the good news of God's Kingdom breaking in on earth, healing the sick and casting out demons. He called some particular guys to be his followers and taught them to do what he was doing. He taught people all over the place, often using parables (stories from ordinary life that contained a deeper meaning), and performed various other miracles. The general public loved most of this, but a lot of the religious leaders opposed him strongly and sought to put an end to him.

During this time, which was about 3 years, he forewarned his close followers that he would be given over to the authorities and put to death, but would rise to life again, something they found hard to grasp. But just as he said, he was arrested after being betrayed by one of his own men, Judas. After a farce of a trial he was sentenced to be put to death by means of crucifixion, a particularly brutal and public manner of execution. He was first of all whipped and scourged, mocked and ridiculed by the Roman soldiers and made to carry a heavy cross to the place of execution known as Calvary. The suffering that Jesus endured would have been horrific. All this, however, was part of God's plan - Jesus himself said that he laid his life down voluntarily.

In the Old Testament the people of Israel would offer sacrifices for their sins, and the night before God rescued them out of captivity in Egypt they were to offer a sacrificial lamb, known as the Passover Lamb (Exodus chapter 12). All this was a shadow of the true sacrifice that God himself would make to 'take away the sins of the world' (John 1:29). But why is this sacrifice necessary?

The problem with us human beings is we all do wrong. Even when we don't want to do certain wrong things, we seem powerless to help ourselves. This is what the Bible calls sin and the power of sin.

Wrongdoing needs forgiveness but it needs more than that. God is a God of love and mercy, but he is also a God of justice. There is a cost involved in our sin, a cost that we can't meet. So God has done this for us with Jesus paying the price for our wrongdoing and taking our punishment for us.

Jesus' death on the cross is the means of us receiving forgiveness, being released from punishment and condemnation, and also the means of breaking the power of sin over our lives. Not only is the power of sin broken, and through that the power of the devil over us, but the very power of death is conquered. Jesus died a real death on the cross, was buried, and on the third day he rose from the dead. He had raised people back to life during his lifetime, but they all died again sometime later. This resurrection was altogether different. He rose victorious over the very power and right of death. You see sin leads to separation from God which ultimately leads to death. Jesus' death has reconciled us to God which means life eternal, and his resurrection is the proof of this victory.

> *"There was once a man who got himself into terrible debt. It didn't happen overnight but mounted up and up over the years. Eventually he owed so much that he could not possibly repay the debt in his lifetime. He lost all he owned and finally had to sell himself into slavery to those he owed the vast sums of money to. One day a man he did not know came by and saw his plight. This stranger paid off the man's debt and released him from slavery. He did not make him his own slave but gave him freedom. The man who had his debt paid off was so grateful to this stranger that he willingly and lovingly served him the rest of his life".*

## Have a look

Look up the following Bible verses and write down the word that the writer uses to describe the meaning of Jesus' death for us, then add something to explain what this means to you.

Mark 10:45 ...................................................................................

...............................................................................................

...............................................................................................

Colossians 1:14 ...........................................................................

...............................................................................................

...............................................................................................

Romans 5:11 ................................................................................

...............................................................................................

...............................................................................................

**Practical Response: Thank God**

Take a little time to thank God for what you now realise Jesus has saved you from. And then ask God to begin to show you what Jesus has saved you for.

**Questions for Reflection:**

1. Why do you think it was necessary for Jesus to die on our behalf?

2. How easy or hard do you find it to receive God's forgiveness? Why do you think that is?

3. If Jesus is risen from the dead, what hope does that give to you?

**\*\*\*\*\*\*\*\*\*\***

### Growth Point:

Begin reading Mark's Gospel, maybe reading one chapter every day, writing down what strikes you, and noting any questions you might have.

**\*\*\*\*\*\*\*\*\*\***

# 3. The Loving Father

*This is your God*

*"Yet to all who did receive him (Jesus), to those who believed in his name, he gave the right to become children of God"*
*- John*

In the Old Testament God revealed himself and was known by the Israelite people by various names over the centuries. Because of the people's hard-heartedness and rebellion, they often failed to truly grasp the heart of God for them. Every now and then people like King David would come forth who knew God in a more intimate way. David understood God as his shepherd which we find expressed in the famous 23$^{rd}$ Psalm. The shepherd cared for, protected and loved his sheep.

Jesus brought the full and complete revelation of God, and the term he constantly used for God was 'Father.' Jesus portrayed God as the loving father that he is, who is intensely interested in our lives and wants to bring out the very best in us.

**However we have two problems with this:**
First, so many people have misunderstood God and still interpret their relationship with him through faulty understanding and wrong models of what God is like. If you think of God as an angry judge then it'll hard for you to see him as a loving father. We need to get

rid of these false understandings in order to embrace the truth that Jesus reveals to us about God.

Second, for some people the term 'father' is not endearing. Their own father may have been absent or abusive. It is vital that we don't judge God as Father by our own experience of an imperfect human father, but that we understand that true fatherhood does in fact come from God. It is necessary to forgive the failings of our own fathers in order to receive the perfect love of our Heavenly Father.

Jesus related to God as his Father and models that relationship for us. He addressed him as 'abba' in his own language of the time. This was a very personal and intimate term that expressed a close, loving relationship of a child to his or her father.

Jesus received his Father's affirmation when on more than one occasion he heard a voice from heaven declare, 'This is my Son, whom I love, with him I am well pleased.' We too can receive that same affirmation, not because we have done great things, but simply because we are now in relationship with Jesus and we too are children of God.

A loving father or mother loves their children for who they are, not for what they do. Think of a small baby. It can do little for its parents but instead keeps them awake at night, demands food and needs to be changed! Yet the parents adore this little one because he or she is theirs, and because of their relationship with the child. So God the Father loves us, even in our immaturity, neediness and through our mistakes. He is patient with us; he does correct us and at times disciplines us as is right and necessary, but always to build us up and never to tear us down.

---

Helen first became a Christian with no church background from her past and knew nothing of what the Bible taught.

*"At first I just came to Jesus and didn't know God as a Father or anything else much about him. As I began to learn about who God really is, and to deal with some of the issues and insecurities of my own life (having not always had a natural father's protection), I began to discover the true Fatherhood of God. This gave me a sense of his love, protection and affirmation of me as his special daughter. I knew a safety of being totally and fully embraced in his arms of love. I began to realise that I could curl up in my heavenly daddy's lap anytime and he never rejects me or is too busy for me. I have this picture of Father God being in front of me, being over me and beside me whenever and wherever I need him to be. It's like he has a big smile on his face and it's just beaming down on me."*

---

**Have a look**

Look up and read the story Jesus told that is in Luke 15:11-32.

Who are the three main characters in this story?

.....................................................................................................

.....................................................................................................

.....................................................................................................

Who do you think they represent?

..........................................................................................

..........................................................................................

..........................................................................................

What do you observe about the father – his attitudes and actions?

..........................................................................................

..........................................................................................

..........................................................................................

## Practical Response: The Father

What was your experience like of being fathered as you grew up? Take some time to consider the good and give thanks for this. Now consider the negative aspects and forgive. You might want to speak out forgiveness for specific things. Think about how you might need to change the way you think about God as Father.

## Questions for Reflection:

1. What do you think are the most important attributes of a father?
2. As a child of God, what do you suppose he thinks about you?
3. What would be some ways for you to get to know God as your Heavenly Father?

\*\*\*\*\*\*\*\*\*\*

**Growth Point:**

Spend time every week with other believers so you can be encouraged in your faith.

\*\*\*\*\*\*\*\*\*\*

# 4. Power for Living

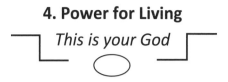

*This is your God*

*"You will receive power when the Holy Spirit comes on you."*
*- Jesus*

The Holy Spirit is the third 'person' of the Godhead along with the Father and the Son, Jesus. He used to be referred to sometimes as the Holy Ghost which gave quite a scary sounding idea of who he is!

When we put our faith in Jesus, he gives us the gift of the Holy Spirit who lives in and with us, enabling us to live the life that Jesus wants for us. He is the gift that we all need.

In the Hebrew language of the Old Testament there is a word that means spirit, and also wind or breath. The Holy Spirit is like the breath of God that breathes life into our souls. He is also like the wind – you don't see him, you can't catch him or control him, but you can feel his effects.

The Holy Spirit is also referred to as the Spirit of Jesus or the Spirit of the Lord. Indeed Jesus himself was filled with and lived in the power of the Spirit. It was through the Holy Spirit that he healed the sick and performed miraculous works.

Jesus described the Holy Spirit as our 'comforter' which meant one who comes alongside us to strengthen us, help us, encourage us and cheer us on. Paul said the Holy Spirit was like a deposit or downpayment in our lives that guaranteed all else that God would give us in Jesus Christ.

## What does the Holy Spirit give to us?

**1. Power to change:** As we come to Jesus, we recognise that we can't live the life God wants for us in our own strength. The Holy Spirit comes and dwells within us, working from the inside out to change us from having a tendency to be self-centred, self-absorbed and maybe even self-righteous, to becoming God-centred and focussed, and he works in us the right living that Jesus has made possible.

**2. Power to live:** The Holy Spirit is our constant companion who strengthens our inner being so that we can know the love of God in a real way on a daily basis. This is what gives us the power to live for God each day. It is important that we develop a relationship with the Holy Spirit so we can keep in step with him as he leads and guides us through all the events and obstacles that come our way.

**3. Power to make Jesus known:** A main purpose of the Holy Spirit's coming is to make Jesus known, and he wants to do that through you. He gives us courage and wisdom to know how to present Jesus to people, and he gives us power to demonstrate what Jesus can do, for example healing people.

## The Fruit of the Spirit

In one of his letters the Apostle Paul lists some of the destructive patterns of behaviour that our 'sinful nature' tends to indulge in or be drawn to. He then contrasts this with a list of the fruit of the

Spirit – love, joy, peace, patience, kindness, goodness, faithfulness, gentleness and self-control. I think you'd prefer people to show you those sorts of things rather than anger, jealousy and so forth. So we should want to display the fruit of the Spirit in our lives. But who can be loving, joyful, peaceful, patient etc? Well none of us could all the time except by the working of the Holy Spirit in us. That's why these characteristics are the fruit, not of us ourselves, but of the Spirit in us. (This can be found in Galatians 5:22-23).

## The Gifts of the Spirit

As the Holy Spirit helps us to serve people effectively and to make Jesus known in the world, he equips us with some very interesting gifts. These are gifts to communicate something from God, and to demonstrate God's power in ways that point to Jesus as Lord.

Some of these gifts are:
**Prophecy** – the ability to receive and communicate a message from God to a person or group of people, primarily for their encouragement and strengthening.
**Healing** – a provision of power from God to release his healing into a person, physically, emotionally or mentally.
**Tongues** – this gift can seem very odd at first, but it is very helpful to us. It is the God-given ability to speak and pray in a heavenly language that, though our mind does not understand it, we are speaking or praying from our spirit. When Jesus' disciples first received the Holy Spirit in power, they all spoke in tongues. (More on these gifts can be found in 1 Corinthians 12:1-11).

## Be filled with the Spirit

So we really need the Holy Spirit on our adventure of following Jesus and our exploration of getting to truly know God the Father. It is important we don't take the Holy Spirit for granted but that we actively seek to be filled with him on a regular basis. When he first fills us, this can be accompanied by the release of gifts in us or a great sense of God's power in our lives.

---

*"When I first became a Christian no-one told me much about the Holy Spirit or the role that he could play in my walk with God. A while later I was at a Christian conference in Brighton on the south coast of England. Here I not only heard about the Holy Spirit, I watched as his power was at work and people were healed. More than that I received prayer with the laying on of hands like in the Bible, and was filled with the Holy Spirit in a wonderful way. I didn't feel much at the time but when I went back to the Bed and Breakfast I was staying at and knelt by the bed to pray, I found myself suddenly gushing forth in an unknown tongue! Even more important, when I returned home my wife, Helen, immediately noticed a significant difference in me for the better. I seemed to her like a different person in some way. Since then I have continued to pray in tongues often, finding this to be a great aid, especially when I don't know what to pray in a situation. I have also from that time been launched into moving in the power of God in healing and other ways."*

---

## Have a look

Look up these verses in the Bible and note down what else the Holy Spirit does for us:

Romans 8:16

.................................................................................................

.................................................................................................

Romans 8:26

.................................................................................................

.................................................................................................

John 14:26

.................................................................................................

.................................................................................................

## Practical Response: Be Filled with Holy Spirit

Ask God to fill you with the Holy Spirit in a dynamic way and release his gifts in you. Believe that God gives good gifts to those who ask and start using what he releases to you. (It might be good to get a couple of Christian leaders to pray for you to be filled with the Holy Spirit).

## Questions for Reflection:

1. How important do you think it is to be filled with the Holy Spirit?
2. What is the main thing you need the Holy Spirit to help you with right now?
3. What is the difference between us trying to be loving, kind,

patient etc. and letting the Holy Spirit work in us to produce that sort of fruit?

*********

**Growth Point:**

Tell someone about Jesus and what he means to you. Trust the Holy Spirit to give you the right words to say to the right person who needs to hear them. As we share our faith with other people our faith is strengthened.

*********

# Part 2 - Your New Life

## *Introduction*

*"I have come so they can have real and eternal life, more and better life than they ever dreamed of"* – Jesus

Despite what some people think, the Christian life is not always easy! It doesn't mean we no longer have troubles, struggle with things, or even cease getting hurt. That was a reality check for me! The Christian life however is an invitation to experience freedom, fullness and to see incredible transformation happen through and in your life. And in the battles, we know God is still who he says he is.

In this part, we will look at three keys that are so essential in your new life with God. Grasping each of these so early on can save possibly years of struggling to feel good enough with God. It stops your past holding you back and hindering you from entering into real freedom to be who you fully are meant to be, something so few individuals (sadly) have experienced. God wants you free and has all this for you now, and you do not need to earn your way to it.

We will be looking at God's love for us and why this is now our foundation for everything else that happens in our lives. We will see why God does not want our past, no matter what we have done, to dictate our future. It is a new day for us! And finally in this section, we will talk about the importance of forgiveness and how this is so vital in our day-to-day life.

# 5. Love is the Standard

*Your New Life*

*"...God is love. This is how God showed his love among us: He sent his one and only Son into the world that we might live through him."*
*– John the Apostle*

One of the greatest revelations in my walk with God is knowing that there is nothing that I can do that can make him love me any more and there is nothing that I can do that would make him love me any less. I am loved by him because of who I am and not because of what I do or don't do. I am loved when I am singing away in church and I am loved when I am sitting watching television. I am loved.

### God is Love and we are Loved

Sometimes God is portrayed in ways where love is not the characteristic you would associate with him. He is sometimes viewed as angry and distant. However this misrepresented image has come from people who do not know him. What we find in Scripture is really a story of love. It is the story of a loving father longing to be in relationship with his children. Despite our failures and our ignorance of him, still God pursues and chases after us.

A story Jesus used to demonstrate this was that of the prodigal son: a son who took his inheritance early from his father and squandered it all on drugs, sex and rock n' roll – well, whatever it would have been back then. After living that lifestyle, he found himself with nothing, feeling alone and hungry. He thought even his father's workmen have more than him now. He wanted to return home but he felt he had brought shame and disappointment to his father. The only way to come home was to work for it. So he set off back home, ready to grovel, ready for the relationship to no longer be the same, ready to be a servant rather than a son. But while he was still a long way off, his father saw him and ran to him, throwing his arms around him, embracing him. The son began saying how sorry and unworthy he was, but the father completely ignored his protests and welcomed his son home, clothed him, and the household had a feast and celebrated that the son who everyone thought was gone, had come home. This is so much the heart of God - loving us even when we get it wrong, picking us back up and still rejoicing over the sight of us.

**'No longer living under law but grace'**
Those are words the Apostle Paul spoke in the book of Romans. Those who live under the law follow strict rules and obligations, having to strive and perform. Some individuals do this in their Christian walk, doing X, Y, Z as they feel the need to gain his approval and his attention, not realising the truth that they already have it. It is here where we need to experience the Father's love - just like in the story of the prodigal son – and where we receive our true identity and worth.

As you step further into your new life, you must realise that love is now the standard. As sons and daughters, no matter what we do he loves us consistently, even if we haven't prayed recently or been to church this week. Now listen to me; I am not saying we should do that. These 2 things are so key on our journey with God. However they are never to be used as our heavenly checklist or used for "ticking the boxes" with God. It is all about love. Just because of who you are and not what you do, you are completed, accepted, loved and even liked by God!

---

*"Despite hearing for so many years that "God loves me" and thinking I believed it, one day after hearing teaching on the love of the Father, I looked at my actions and thoughts and realised that I was living life in a way where I was trying to earn God's love. I felt the need to follow a number of steps to gain his favour and attention. When I hadn't done certain things, I came under a tremendous sense of shame and guilt. I realised I had not been living under love but rather had put standards and measures in place in my life that really were not from God. These came partly because I saw my heavenly Father the way I saw my earthly father. My dad is a good father, however at times he is a bit of a perfectionist. So growing up I was always feeling the need to constantly do better in everything I was doing, especially school. I had transferred this into my relationship with God until I really began to grasp that "God really loves me". It is not dependent on what I do; it is just simply because of who I am. It is so much easier to live from that place!"* - Geoffrey

**Have a Look**

Look up the following verses from the Bible and write down what you believe to be the key thing God is saying through them:

*Romans 8:1*  ........................................................................
........................................................................
........................................................................
........................................................................

*Psalm 139:17-18* ....................................................................
........................................................................
........................................................................
........................................................................

*John 15:9*  ........................................................................
........................................................................
........................................................................
........................................................................

**Practical Response: Soak in his Love**

We need to know this not just in our heads but also in our hearts. Take time with God, just being still, reflecting over these verses and letting them go deep into your heart so that you experience more of the love of the Father. What is he saying to you today?

**Questions for Reflection:**

1. What difference does it make to your life, knowing that you are loved simply because of who you are, not because of anything you have done?

2. Is this hard to really believe? Are there things in the way that would stop you from believing this?

3. In what way does this change how you view yourself?

**\*\*\*\*\*\*\*\*\***

**Growth Point:**

Print a copy of the "Father's Love Letter" (available free online at www.fathersloveletter.com). Throughout this week, take time to read over it to hear the words the Father speaks over you. Put it in a place where you will regularly see it, whether it is somewhere at home, work or even in the car, so that you never forget that love is the standard.

**\*\*\*\*\*\*\*\*\***

## 6. Your Past is not Your Future

*Your New Life*

*"Therefore, if anyone is in Christ, he is a new creation, the old has gone, the new has come" – Paul the Apostle*

Many of us are impacted as a result of events that have happened in our past. We can now view life through the lenses that we have formed over the years as a result of these experiences and at times it can cause us problems. For example, words that have been spoken over us by key figures in our lives can negatively impact how we view ourselves and how we approach life. Many of us have been told that we will not amount to much or are insignificant, and as a result of the power of these words, we believe this to be true. In addition to this, there may be experiences we have had that make it difficult for us to trust people because of times when we have been hurt. We may have memories that cause us trauma in our life that we just cannot seem to move on from. These can be really deep and therefore difficult for us to share. However as we enter our new life, God is looking to heal those things that may try to keep us down.

### What does God say?

Constantly what we see throughout Scripture is that when we come to God he offers a new hope and a new day for us. That means that the old has passed away and it is a time to no longer dwell on the past but live in the new life that God has given us. Paul says in the book of Philippians, it's about "forgetting the past and looking forward to what lies ahead". However, it is not just about coming to God and completely ignoring the past. It is about the Father healing you from things that have happened so that you can come to know true forgiveness, freedom and fullness of life. Colossians 1:13-14 says that "God rescued us from dead-end alleys and dark dungeons. He's set us up in the kingdom of the Son he loves so much, the Son who got us out of the pit we were in, got rid of the sins we were doomed to keep repeating". We need to come into the truth of that.

**New way of thinking**
One of the things that is critical in not allowing your past to negatively impact your new life in God is gaining a new way of thinking, that is a transformation of the mind. Our minds are really the control centres for our entire beings. One of the enemy's main ways to keep us stuck is by suggesting thoughts into our heads that are contrary to God's truth, as this is the way to impact our behaviour and our actions. For example, it may be that someone is plagued with thoughts of rejection. Maybe they have been rejected in the past by family or friends and throughout life, so there is a constant tape that plays in their head, "You shouldn't open up to people because you are just going to get hurt". As a result, the individual does not allow others to get alongside or close to them. They feel isolated and alone in life, but due to the risk of rejection, it seems better that way. As you can see, something in the past that someone has experienced can have a serious impact on the way an individual lives their life and as a result we can feel trapped.

## Cast off the Past

Take hold of what the Apostle Paul said: "The new has come". It is what you are entitled to in your new life. The power of the cross means that everything from our past can be wiped away. Jesus cried out on the cross "It is finished!" However we must take hold of it so that we apply what He has accomplished. Keys for this are understanding what God has done for us, asking God to heal us from past experiences and making sure that we develop a new way of thinking which is based on the truth God speaks over us.

*"My childhood was a huge rollercoaster. My father was absent; I had times in a children's home, and a difficult relationship with my mother. At seventeen I became pregnant and my son was given up for adoption. The following years featured many relationships, three marriages, drug-taking and costly visits to fortune tellers and clairvoyants. I had no self-respect, self-esteem or confidence.*

*That was my past but it's gone – done and dusted. I came to Jesus and found the love of Father God who over the years has healed, restored and transformed me. My relationship with God the Father has grown in ways I never thought possible. It's a new journey of faith and understanding, and I'm excited about life again. His word says to me, "Forget the things of the past, look I'm doing a new thing." - Julie*

## Have a Look

Look up the following verses and see what God gives us when we come to him. What does that mean to you?

*Ezekiel 36:26* .......................................................................
...........................................................................................
...........................................................................................
...........................................................................................

*1 Peter 1:3* .........................................................................
...........................................................................................
...........................................................................................
...........................................................................................

*Ephesians 4:23* ...................................................................
...........................................................................................
...........................................................................................
...........................................................................................

## Practical Response: Allowing God to Heal

Take some quiet time with God and reflect on whether there is anything you feel God may want to speak to you about from the past. Take time in his presence and allow him to heal you from past hurts and ask God to reveal where he was in each of these situations.

## Questions for Reflection

1. In what way do you resonate with what has been written?

2. Why do you think people find it difficult letting go of the past?

3. What do you believe your future holds now you are with God?

**\*\*\*\*\*\*\*\*\*\***

### Growth Point:

To develop a new way of thinking, every time a thought comes into your mind that is something that would oppose the truth of God in your life, immediately speak out loud in prayer for a family member or friend to come into a relationship with God. The negative thoughts might not immediately stop but they may come less often as the enemy will know this is a strategy not to use on you.

**\*\*\*\*\*\*\*\*\*\***

# 7. The Power of Forgiveness

*Your New Life*

*"...Bear with each other and forgive what other grievances you may have against one another. Forgive as the Lord forgave you..." – Paul the Apostle*

Forgiveness is not always an easy act and because of this it is not something we regularly see occur in society. It's the reason for many broken relationships, broken families and in turn many broken lives. Loads of self-help books that we see filling our bookstores highlight the importance of forgiveness in being vital to maintaining good health and peace of mind. However this is not a new discovery... the Bible has been saying it for centuries! Forgiveness is a principle that we see repeatedly mentioned in Scripture in order to live a free life. Being unwilling or unable to forgive is one of the major barriers that stands in the way of many Christians finding effective solutions to problems; not only to receiving healing, but to finding fulfilment and satisfaction, finding peace and receiving the blessing of God. In addition, unforgiveness can build up within you, resulting in bitterness and even physical ill-health.

## Why you need to forgive

Jesus does not hold back when it comes to talking about the importance of forgiveness. When speaking to a large crowd he said "For if you forgive other people when they sin against you, your heavenly Father will also forgive you. But if you do not forgive others of their sins, your Father will not forgive you". Therefore it is very clear; if we do not forgive, the Father cannot forgive us for what we have done. At another point Jesus teaches us that unforgiveness will cause us to be and feel trapped. In the parable of the unmerciful servant in Matthew 18, Jesus tells the story of a servant whose debt was cancelled by his master. The debt was the equivalent to 20 annual salaries! Despite having the debt waived, the servant demanded the money he was owed from a fellow worker (only a day's wage!) However the poor man was unable to pay and therefore the servant had him put in jail. After the master heard this, he called upon the servant. He couldn't believe that despite the mercy that was shown to him, he didn't show it to others. So the master responded angrily and handed the servant over to the jailers so that he too would be there until he paid back all he owed. Jesus told this story to demonstrate how the Father would treat us if we didn't forgive. We would be trapped in our own sinfulness and would miss out on the benefits that we are entitled to in our new life with him.

**Misconceptions on Forgiveness**
Individuals can have some misconceptions on what forgiveness really means. The first misunderstanding is that before it can occur, you must "feel" like forgiving the individual. But forgiveness is actually a choice that we need to make. Some of the things that have happened in people's lives are really horrendous, so of course there is no way they feel like forgiving. We must make a choice to forgive and God never asks us to do something without him, without his power or his grace. We just need to come to the cross to

remind ourselves of what he has done for us, so that we are able to forgive others. What happens when this takes place is that it allows God to heal those wounds from the past even more and he is able to pour more and more of himself and his love into us.

The second misunderstanding is that forgiveness condones what has happened or what has been done to you. The truth is that forgiveness liberates us. We are not saying what happened was acceptable, because it was not. Forgiving someone allows you to unbind that emotional ball and chain that you have been dragging around for a long time and there are now no ties or obligations between you and the person you have forgiven. They are still answerable for what they have done. However rather than to you, they are now answerable just to God. Forgiveness is such a key and it unlocks so much freedom in our life and in our experience where there has been a painful issue, whether it is physical, emotional, or spiritual. As a result of forgiveness being given, things are changed in an instant and often the process of healing really begins. So, forgive those who wrong you, no matter what has happened, no matter who it is - a friend, someone you really struggle with, or even yourself! Remember and let God help you through the process of choosing to forgive.

*"I was consumed by hatred towards my father for all that had occurred through my life. To compensate for my anger towards him I threw myself into other things. Outwardly my life looked great, inside I was very unhappy. I completed a degree, was working full-time as a senior manager, owned a lovely flat, and had a great social life.*

*One particular weekend sticks out. I was at a party and spent the night vomiting as I had drunk so much alcohol. When morning came I was utterly desperate to go home, I just felt dirty and horrid. After this night I snapped and became seriously unwell with depression and anxiety. I had a mental breakdown. I had to give up work and stopped going to church.*

*Life was utterly intolerable. I lived in a bottomless, desolate pit. I had little energy. I slept night and day but my sleep was plagued with terrifying nightmares. I had frequent psychiatrist appointments and was on massive quantities of medication that seemed to do little. This went on for several years.*

*One Sunday I decided to go to a local church. I walked in the church door and the peace that descended on me was indescribable. I opened my heart up to Jesus, people prayed with me and my depression just disappeared. My doctors were astounded. My psychiatrist told me in January I would not be able to live and work within the foreseeable future. However, by April I was discharged from the psychiatrist and by October I had been offered another job.*

*Although I wasn't depressed I still struggled and required a maintenance dose of antidepressant to keep me stable. I received counselling and healing prayer and have forgiven my dad, such that I can now feel love towards him. I have also forgiven myself for my sinful lifestyle. This forgiveness is absolutely essential to my complete healing. I have now been deemed fit by my doctor to stop the maintenance drugs".* - Karen

**Have a look**

Look up the following verses and write down what you discover about forgiveness and what it means for your life:

*Matthew 18:21-22*.......................................................................................

..........................................................................................

..........................................................................................

..........................................................................................

*Mark 11:25*      .......................................................................................

..........................................................................................

..........................................................................................

..........................................................................................

*Matthew 6:14-16* .......................................................................................

..........................................................................................

..........................................................................................

..........................................................................................

**Practical Response: Forgiving Others**

Take some time with God and ask him to search your heart to see whether there is anyone you need to forgive in your life. For each person that comes to mind, speak out the forgiveness and release them from what they have done or said to you. "I choose to forgive......for......"

**Questions for Reflection:**

1. What stops you from forgiving someone? What makes it difficult at times?

2. What do you now see as the consequences of choosing not to forgive someone?

3. How would society look if many more began adopting continual forgiveness as a value?

\*\*\*\*\*\*\*\*\*

**Growth Point:**

As you continue to live in a way which forgives, encourage one person close to you to do the same. Let them know the difference it has made in your life and tell them the importance of it for their own life.

\*\*\*\*\*\*\*\*\*

## Part 3 – Your New Identity

### Introduction

*"Jesus came back, "God bless you, Simon, son of Jonah!... My Father in heaven, God himself, let you in on this secret of who I really am. And now I'm going to tell you who you are, really are. You are Peter, a rock"* – Jesus

Our whole world is going through an identity crisis. Individuals do not know who they really are. Many are searching for their true self and are looking in various places to discover what this might be. As we come to God, he brings about who we truly are. We have a new identity in Christ. No longer should our own negative thoughts and what people have spoken over us determine what we can be or do. The Father now defines us.

In Scripture, there are a number of occasions where God changed people's names. As a result, a shift took place in each person's life and they began to walk more fully into God's plan for them. Simon was not an apostle until he was named Peter. Saul became Paul, signalling a change in who he was. Abram had his name changed to Abraham which meant "father of the nations," and from that time on, he was able to step even more into who he was created to be. His wife had her name changed from Sarai to Sarah, the mother of nations.

We are not saying that God will change what we are known by. For example, "James, you are now to be called Geoffrey!" What God does is tell us our true identity, what we can become and what we can achieve. Negative names will hold us down whereas great names will release power into our lives and bring about the purposes of God. The Father is speaking these over us.

Just like Jesus in the desert in Luke chapter 4, at times our identity may be challenged. However God is looking for us to discover and enter in to who we are, so that we cannot be shaken, no matter what is going on round about us.

## 8. Do I now need to become a saint?

*Your New Identity*

*"...to the saints ... the faithful in Christ Jesus"*
*– Paul the Apostle*

In my experience, one of the concerns individuals have in following Jesus is an uncertainty about whether they are good enough to live the Christian life. There seems to be an expectation that you must now live perfectly. There is no room for error and you must become some sort of saint.

Alongside having love as our standard, we must come into the realisation of the changes that have taken place in our identity. Part of this is a shift from being known as a sinner to becoming a saint. This may sound strange, however when we look at Scripture, this is what God calls us. When we turn our hearts towards him and invite him into our lives, our new identity comes. Before we received Christ, we were called sinners - characters prone to sin. However, because of the power of the cross, we have become righteous in his eyes. We are now viewed as saints. The term is defined as "holy believers". When Paul was writing to other followers in his letters, he often referred to them with this title. They did not earn that position through years of doing good works, as we associate with many of the modern-day saints. It was simply the status God gave them.

This is true for us today. We are no longer just "sinners saved by grace". We have become the "righteousness of God", without sin or guilt. If you still believe you are a sinner then maybe that is all you are going to become. Proverbs 23:7 shows the importance again on our thoughts: "As a man thinks within himself, so he is". Believing you are only a sinner may cause you to stay trapped in cycles of sin. As saints, we now believe that it is below our nature to act like that. God has better for us. It obviously does not mean that we become incapable of committing sin, but its power over our lives is broken. "We are now dead to sin" (Romans 6:2). We must believe the truth of that so that we see the reality of it in our lives.

## Holiness

Holiness may seem like a term that is very outdated for this generation. In some cases, the concept has many negative connotations. However it is very much a Scriptural idea. Some may associate it with a list of do's and don'ts, certain mannerisms or simply just unattainable perfection. In the book of Leviticus, God says, "Be holy, as I am holy." It means to be separated from sin and given fully to God. Holiness is an invitation to come into a deeper relationship with God and as a result become more and more like Jesus. This must therefore challenge us to look at our lives and see whether there is anything that may be hindering us from this. If we are aware of something, then we have to repent from that action or way of thinking. Furthermore, we should ask God for his strength to see it put to death in our lives. There is no shame or guilt in any of this. Even several years down the line, I am still repenting for things! It is about us realising our new identity so that we are able to see freedom and fullness in our own lives, our relationships and relationship with God.

There are three key ways we can see this part of our identity reinforced:

- Developing our secret place with God: Spending time with him. The key is focusing on him, not our own shortcomings. We become what we behold.
- Living in community: being around other believers who can encourage and support us in our new life.
- Being part of the kingdom advancing: stepping into the plans that God has for our lives.

Each of these can bring a different dynamic that can allow you to step even more fully into the reality that you are now a saint and that sin has no permission to hold you down.

> *"I used to wear a mask on the outside but inside I was a mess. My life was a series of one night stands, taking ecstasy and other drugs as well as supplying them. I broke the law, stole from shops and lied to my family. There were so many situations where I put my life at risk and thoughts of suicide went around in my head.*
>
> *I had a deep desire to confess my wrongdoing and one day visited a church where I wept uncontrollably. I poured out my darkest secrets to a woman from the church. She simply took my hands and said, "Jesus loves you." I gave my heart to Jesus and came home to my heavenly Father who has given me a new life – a life worth living. I am free from all my past and now have true life that I can live to the full." - Andrea*

**Have a Look**

Look up Romans 6:1-14. Write down what you discover about your new identity and some of the keys for stepping into the truth of it.

...........................................................................................................
...........................................................................................................
...........................................................................................................
...........................................................................................................
...........................................................................................................
...........................................................................................................
...........................................................................................................
...........................................................................................................
...........................................................................................................

.........................................................................................

.........................................................................................

.........................................................................................

**Practical Response: Rising Above**

Take some time to think about what has been written in this chapter. Is there anything in your life that may be a hindrance to walking in greater freedom and fullness? Are there sinful thoughts or actions that you need God's strength to overcome? Speak to God about them. Ask him to give you the power to rise above each of these and for you to realise your identity as a saint.

**Questions for Reflection:**

1. What do you think of when you hear the term "saint"?
2. How does this identity change make you feel?
3. What do you believe to be the key things in pursuing "holiness"?

**\*\*\*\*\*\*\*\*\*\***

**Growth Point:**

Print a copy of "Who I am in Christ" (available from www.ficm.org and many other websites). This holds a number of statements relating to our new identity in Christ. Start each morning this week by declaring each of these sentences out loud over yourself. Understanding who we are and living from that place will release greater freedom in our lives.

**\*\*\*\*\*\*\*\*\*\***

## 9. Arise Princes and Princesses

*Your New Identity*

*"Now if we are Children, then we are heirs – heirs of God and co-heirs with Christ."*
*– Paul the Apostle*

As we become children of God, another realisation that must take place is that we are now seated with Christ (Ephesians 2:6). We have effectively become princes and princesses in the eyes of heaven.  This must cause us to reconsider our true worth and significance, impacting how we view ourselves and how we live life.

**Your worth**

In everyday life, we gain (or fail to gain) our sense of worth from a wide range of sources. It may be from our own personal achievements or from other people's opinions. This can have a positive or negative effect on how we feel about ourselves and about life. For some, it can cause pride and arrogance. For others, it can leave them with feelings of worthlessness and insignificance. From our own sets of relationships, we may be able to see this in others or even in our own lives. We see examples in Scripture as well. Some relied on their own strength and let over-confidence come into their hearts. At times the disciples were in danger of doing this. In Luke 9, Jesus caught them arguing about which one of them would become the greatest. Also, some often turned too far in the other direction. Individuals lost confidence in who God had called them to be and it caused them to miss out on the fullness he was offering. It happened with the Israelites when they were trying to first enter the Promised Land. They looked at the impossible situation and had lost focus on what God had said. As a result, none of that generation saw the promise fulfilled.

## Keeping a Right Perspective

God reveals to us where we should draw our value from. It is through who he has created us to be and what he has done for us. Firstly, our value should come from the fact that we have been fearfully and wonderfully made (Psalm 139:14). When he was planning the creation of the world, he had you in mind. Many live feeling like they were a mistake; however he planned the exact date and time of your birth. It was not an accident. He took time over you and knitted you together in your mother's womb.

Secondly, our value is shown through Jesus' death. When we think we are worthless, we should remember again how much God paid to be in relationship with us. He sent his only son into the world - a man who was humiliated, beaten, and later nailed to a cross. For some, Mel Gibson's "Passion of the Christ" is very distressing to watch, but it gives us an idea of the pain and agony Jesus went through. I sometimes think it must have been even more difficult for the Father to watch. He could have stepped in at any time. However, because of the price that had to be paid, he allowed it to happen. If it was only to be in relationship with just you, he would have still gone through with it. That is how much you are worth!

Finally, our value should come through knowing we have a purpose. We were not born so life could pass us by: we were born for significance. You were created for something no one else in this world can do. No one else can fulfil the plans that God has for you. These are plans to prosper you and not to harm you. Therefore in your new identity, let God determine your worth and value. Listening to and believing negative sources will cause you to miss out on the truth.

> "I had grown up in an environment where I perceived that much was expected of me and where I felt most valued and loved when I lived up to these expectations and excelled.  The problem was that my understanding of why people loved me became skewed and eventually it did not matter what they thought because I never felt satisfied with myself.  As a young teacher in a highly successful and academic school, my need to perform and achieve intensified.  Unable to resolve my own need for validation and worth in my work, ministry or relationships, I became dangerously ill with an eating disorder and the associated depression. Thankfully in the midst of this I never let go of my experience of God's presence and the truth of the Scriptures.  I never doubted that my hope and healing would be found in Him; I just had no idea how to get there.  It was in the context of relationship where people came alongside me and loved me that this healing began.  For the first time I had a Christian leader invite me into relationship to 'be' rather than 'do', and I had friends who knew I had nothing to give, but who still wanted to make time to be with me and include me in their lives.  These people and many who have now joined them have taught me what I knew the Scriptures said but could not get without an experience to relate them to.  They showed me that it was possible to be loved and have value before I ever did anything to deserve it.  This opened a door for me to experience how God loves and values me."- Jeanette

## Have a Look

Look up the following verses and write down how they make you feel about yourself:

*Psalm 139:13-16* ..............................................................................
.............................................................................................
.............................................................................................
.............................................................................................

*Ephesians 1:3-8* ...............................................................................
.............................................................................................
.............................................................................................
.............................................................................................

*Jeremiah 29:11-12* .............................................................................
.............................................................................................
.............................................................................................
.............................................................................................

**Practical Response: Realising your Worth**

Write down where you currently draw your worth from. Ask God to help you see if there are any lies you have believed about yourself in this area. Ask him to help you come into the truth of what he says.

.............................................................................................
.............................................................................................
.............................................................................................
.............................................................................................

**Questions for Reflection:**

1. How does hearing all this make you feel about yourself?
2. What changes do you see happening, if any?

3. Is it difficult at times to hold onto the truth of what God says? Why is that the case?

**\*\*\*\*\*\*\*\*\***

### Growth Point:

Consider the way you speak to people and the things you say. Are you making them feel valued by your words? Do they feel valued after spending time with you? Resolve today to be a person who 'adds worth' to others.

**\*\*\*\*\*\*\*\*\***

# 10. Celebrating who you are

*Your New Identity*

*"Your hands shaped me and made me"*
*– Job*

After God made you, he threw away the mould. He created us each with a unique flavour and style. Each of us has our own set of skills, gifts and abilities. When we look around, there is no one that is identical to us. Walking through a busy city centre, you will be able to see a wide range of sometimes peculiar individuals with varying fashion senses, hairstyles, looks, sizes and voices. God loves variety. This can make life's relationships difficult at times, as others do not think the same way we do. I sometimes think situations would be easier if people thought more like me. But then how dull would this place be if we were all the same?

When we step into our new identity in Christ, God does not want us to lose our unique flavour. It is not his idea that we all become clones of one another. We may feel the need to fit into a certain picture of how a Christian should be, speak and act. However, we will struggle to do so. That is because he created each of us to bring a fresh expression of who he is to this world and not to be a replica.

Many pray: "God, all of you and none of me or less of me". It is a well-intended prayer: however before you were created, there was less of you. God didn't like that idea, so he made you. He celebrates who we are therefore does not want to see your flavour diminished. There may be things in your life you know God wants to work on, but I would question whether those things were really you and part of your true identity.

## Why should I?

Knowing that we are able to be who we are allows us so much freedom in our lives. No more striving to become someone we are not and no more striving to fit into that specific Christian mould. This should be liberating for us. Our thoughts will no longer be consumed with how we can become better than we are. Our focus will lift from ourselves and will leave more room for our eyes to be more on God. This is how we become everything we have been created to be.

## How can I do this?

### A – Acknowledge who you are

Take time to acknowledge who you are. Ask questions such as: 'Who am I really? What makes me, me? What are my strengths?'

### B – Be who you are

Many have drifted away from who they are because of different circumstances and situations in their lives. At times it is easier to be someone different. As men and women in Scripture stepped into who they were, God's purposes for their lives began to unfold.

### C – No longer compare yourselves with others

Many of us are guilty of this. We compare ourselves to others, maybe longing to be more like someone in a certain way and at times, wishing we would make progress in life as they do. What is true is that measuring up only causes us to get down. We need to be setting our own "personal bests."

Never lose your flavour and embrace who you have been created to be.

---

"When I first began to get involved at a leadership capacity in my church, I took a look at who I was. I realised I brought a lot of humour to everything I was involved in. I felt that it sometimes ruined deep spiritual moments and I just couldn't stay serious all the time. It used to really bother me. So much so in fact, I had a conversation with God about it. By becoming a leader I felt I had to become much more "mature". I said to him "God, I no longer want to be seen as the funny guy". It seems silly in hindsight; however it was what I wanted. In the coming weeks, I tried so hard to become what I thought was more "mature" but I was struggling. A couple of weeks after having this conversation with God I went to a teaching conference. During one of the sessions the speaker had a prophetic word for me. He said "I see you dressed as a clown. You are born to be a funny guy. As a result of your humour you will allow people to feel part of the church family and will allow others to come in and experience it". God was answering my prayer. He was saying he didn't want to take my humour away as that was who he created me to be. As a result of this time, I now feel free to be me!"

---

## Have a Look

Read the story of Gideon's call in Judges 6:11-15. He later went on to defeat Israel's enemy with only 300 men. Reflect on the passage mentioned:

What did God say Gideon's true identity was?

.............................................................................................................

.............................................................................................................

What concerns did Gideon have?

.............................................................................................................

.............................................................................................................

.............................................................................................................

How can you relate with Gideon?

.............................................................................................................

.............................................................................................................

.............................................................................................................

## Practical Response: Your Identity

Take time to thank God for who he has created you to be. Ask him the question: "How do you view me today God?" Wait for a response. You may receive or sense an answer. It is usually much better than something we can think up! Learn to keep a record of what God speaks to you so that you don't forget.

## Questions for Reflection:

1. What do you think are the key things that make you unique? What do you feel you bring to situations that others don't?

2. Are there situations and places where you feel you can't be yourself? How does it make you feel?

3. What has struck you from your reading in this whole section regarding your new identity?

**\*\*\*\*\*\*\*\*\*\***

### Growth Point:

Look for somewhere to volunteer where you are able to give some of your time and abilities. Could you serve at your church in some way or could you find another Christian charity to help out with?

**\*\*\*\*\*\*\*\*\*\***

## Part 4 – Developing a Secret Place with God

*Introduction*

In Matthew chapter 6 Jesus talks about giving to the needy and praying. He points out the weakness of those who make a big show of their giving and praying, who do it in a way to draw attention and applause from people. In contrast to that, Jesus tells us to give in secret so only God and ourselves know, and to pray in the secret place.

As we seek to grow in our relationship with God and go a little deeper, it is important to develop this secret place with him – a quiet, undisturbed place where we can have time alone with the Lord. This 'place' is a heart attitude rather than a location.

Four important ways to build this in our lives are through prayer; worship (praise and thanksgiving to God); studying God's Word, the Bible; and listening to God's voice as he communicates with us in various ways.

Just as seeds grow in the dark, unseen place under the soil, so we grow deep roots in God in the secret place. This not only brings steady and lasting growth, but also gives us a secure place in difficult and troublesome times.

## 11. Prayer: It's What Changes Things

*The Secret Place*

*"Jesus often withdrew to lonely places and prayed"*
*— Luke*

We've probably all prayed at sometime, even if we didn't really know what we were doing or who, if anyone, we were talking to. The most common prayer in those situations is usually a very short one – 'Help!'

**So what is prayer and how do we pray?**
Prayer is communication with God – and it's two-way! It is a natural expression of our relationship just as we would talk with friends, parents, children, husband or wife. Prayer expresses our delight in God (and he delights in us), as well as our dependence on God. So it's not all asking for things, though it is OK to do that. God does want us to ask him for what we need, but it is more than that. Sometimes it can be just sitting still, being aware that he is always with us.

**Some different types of prayer:**
We might use the following terms to describe various types of prayer. The Bible says to 'pray in the Spirit on all occasions with all kinds of prayer' (Ephesians 6:18).

**Personal Petitions** – this is where we ask our heavenly Father for what we need, for our 'daily bread.' This may be for material needs, or for strength, peace or wisdom. Talk to God about what you need for each day.

**Devotional Prayer** – this might include simply taking time to adore the Lord, and telling him that we appreciate and love him just as he first loved us.

**Praying for others** – prayer should not be all centred round ourselves, but we should pray for the needs of other people and for our world. We can pray for God to bring justice into situations or for the Holy Spirit to influence people in God's ways.

**Listening Prayer** – remember it's two-way. We'll come back to this in chapter 14.

### How do I pray?
Simply and naturally! Be yourself with God – he knows exactly what you are like anyway. Don't think you need to use special words and pray long, impressive sounding prayers. It's quite the opposite. Jesus said we would not be heard because of our long prayers but God hears us when we approach him with a humble heart.

Jesus has opened the way for us to come right into the Father's presence, and the Holy Spirit helps us to know how and what to pray. If you have received the gift of tongues then use that often in your prayer time in the secret place. It is important that we pray in the following 3 ways: (Mark 11:24-25).

**With Faith** – believing that God hears us and answers us (even if it's not always the way we want or expect).

**With Forgiveness** – not holding anything against another person.

**With Fasting -** Jesus also spoke in Matthew 6 about fasting in the secret place. Fasting is voluntarily going without food (or it could be something like television or e-mails!) for a short period of time in order to focus more fully on seeking God. To fast for a first time you might just miss one meal once a week and give that time to pray for a particular need or situation. There can be great power in prayer with fasting.

You can pray anytime, in fact you can pray all the time. But it is helpful to set aside a special time alone with God on a very regular basis. There is great benefit in prayer as not only does God amazingly and graciously answer prayer, but as we spend time in prayer we ourselves are often changed, and sometimes we become the answer to our own prayers.

> *"Over many years now I have seen God answer prayer. (Unless an incredible amount of coincidences started happening in my life when I started praying!) Helen and I have on many occasions witnessed the Lord providing just what we needed and asked him for. On one occasion, when I was a student and we had two young children to care for, we had no money available to buy food. Helen asked her Father in heaven to provide just £10 so we could feed the children until the next week when we were due some allowance money. No-one else but Helen knew of her prayer that day. Later on that afternoon a small envelope came through our letter box – it contained nothing but a £10 note! God cares about the big issues but also about the little things in our lives"*

**Have a Look**

Look up the prayer that Jesus taught us (the Lord's Prayer as it is often called) in Matthew 6:9-13. Write out the prayer, then re-write it using your own words of what you think the different phrases mean for your life.

...................................................................................................
...................................................................................................
...................................................................................................
...................................................................................................
...................................................................................................
...................................................................................................

..............................................................................................

..............................................................................................

..............................................................................................

..............................................................................................

..............................................................................................

..............................................................................................

## Practical Response: Pray

Write down the things that concern you at this time of your life and talk to your heavenly Father about these things.

..............................................................................................

..............................................................................................

..............................................................................................

..............................................................................................

..............................................................................................

## Questions for Reflection:

1. Have you experienced any answers to prayer? What were they?
2. Why do you think it is important to pray in different ways?
3. Why do you think it is important to pray with faith?

*********

### Growth Point:

Pray for someone you know who really needs Jesus in their life. Ask God to show himself to them and pray for them that they would become aware of God's love for them.

*********

# 12. Living the Lifestyle of Worship

## *The Secret Place*

*"Worship the Lord with gladness; come before him with joyful songs. Enter his gates with thanksgiving and his courts with praise; give thanks to him and praise his name. For the Lord is good and his love endures forever; his faithfulness continues through all generations."*
*– King David*

To worship God is to recognise who he is and to express to him something of his worth. In the Book of Revelation we are given a glimpse into heaven where those around God's throne cry out, "You are worthy, our Lord and God, to receive glory and honour and power."

To worship is to honour God and we can do that with every part of our lives. We honour God by caring for a person in need, so that is actually an act of worship. However we dishonour God when we engage in something like gossip.

**Praise and Thanksgiving:**
Two main expressions of worship are praise and thanksgiving. We praise God for who he is – our Creator, the King of Kings, our Father etc. We thank God for what he does – his provision, his guidance, protection and so forth. So why is it important to worship God in these ways?

God does not need our praise; it's not like we can add anything to him or his value. But as we praise God it enables us to focus on him and his greatness, and it gives us a perspective on life and its challenges in the light of God's awesome power.

God doesn't need our thanks but it seems only right to thank him for what he has done for us, especially in what Jesus has done by dying on the cross for us. Again thanksgiving really does something for us. It helps remove negativity from our minds. It shifts us away from complaining about what's wrong and helps us focus instead on what is right. Praise and thanksgiving release joy into our lives. So even if we don't feel like praising God or giving thanks, when we do so, it lifts our spirits and changes our attitude.

**God is good and his love endures forever:**
The Bible calls us to give thanks in all circumstances. How can we do that? Even in difficult times God's goodness has not changed. When we go through trials God doesn't love us any less. His love, goodness and faithfulness never change. The changing situations of our lives do not alter the truth of God's love for you and his goodness towards you. When we praise and thank God in difficult moments, it can really lift us to a new perspective and bring about real change. Sometimes it is in the most trying circumstances that God works the most amazing things in our lives. When the Apostles Paul and Silas were in a dark dungeon in a prison they were praying and singing hymns of praise at midnight. As they did this, God responded by sending an earthquake that broke open the prison doors. The result

was the jailor and his family came to faith in Jesus, and Paul and
Silas were released.

## How can we make worship a lifestyle?

1. Start each day with praise and thanks recognising that this day
holds all sorts of possibilities in the Lord.

2. Remind yourself that God is with you; be conscious of his
presence throughout your day.

3. Thank God at meal times for his goodness.

4. Ask yourself if what you are doing with your day is honouring to
God or not. (Doing a good job in your workplace is honouring to
God).

5. Finish the day with thanks and ask God to speak to your heart
even through the night.

---

*"Some days in life go really well and others – well, you wish you
hadn't got out of bed. When things go wrong we have a choice – we
can complain and be grumpy or we can choose to praise God
anyway and see what he might make out of our struggles.*

*In some of the most difficult moments of my life, I have found
strength to praise God and not allow bitterness to get hold of me. I
can look back on those times and see that they became the times of
the greatest growth of character in my life."*

---

## Have a Look

Look up Psalm 100 which we quoted at the start. Go through the whole Psalm and write down the different ways it gives of how we can express worship to God; and write down the reasons it gives of why we would appreciate, praise and thank him.

Ways of Praising God

.................................................................................................

.................................................................................................

.................................................................................................

.................................................................................................

.................................................................................................

.................................................................................................

Reasons for Praising God

.................................................................................................

.................................................................................................

.................................................................................................

.................................................................................................

.................................................................................................

.................................................................................................

## Practical Response: 23rd Psalm

Read the 23rd Psalm and use its phrases as a starting point to praise and thank God for who he is and what he does for you.

## Questions for Reflection:

1. Why is it important to give thanks to God?
2. What do you have to give him thanks for?

3. What would help you to be more aware of God's presence throughout the day?

**\*\*\*\*\*\*\*\*\*\***

**Growth Point:**

Try to start every day this week by thanking God for something. Get hold of some good worship music and play it at times in your home, your car or wherever is practical.

**\*\*\*\*\*\*\*\*\*\***

# 13. Feeding on the Word of God

*The Secret Place*

*"Let the word of Christ dwell in you richly"*
*– Paul the Apostle*

Like many people I enjoy a good meal. A good meal for me should always consist of a bit of variety, including something sweet! Reading and studying the Bible can be likened to feeding ourselves well. There are different courses; there is time to have a diet of milk, time to move on to meatier stuff, and of course you'll find something sweet in there too!

## What is the Bible?
The Bible (also referred to as the Scriptures or Word of God) is not so much a book, but a collection of 66 different books that we believe are all inspired by God. (See the appendix at the end of the book which explains a little about each book).

***The Old Testament*** contains 39 books mainly dealing with the history of the people of Israel, and the way God revealed himself to them, related with them and spoke to them through the prophets like Isaiah and Jeremiah.

***The New Testament*** has 27 books – the four Gospels which tell of Jesus' life, death and resurrection, the Acts of the Apostles, letters written by the apostles (often dealing with specific issues) and the book of Revelation (which is a bit mystical but assures us of God's ultimate victory over evil).

The Bible is the unfolding story of God's plan for saving us, with Jesus as the central character.

### Why should you read the Bible?
1. It will help you get to know more about God and his ways, and draw closer to him.
2. It will increase your faith. Faith comes by hearing the Word of God.
3. God will speak to us as we read his Word.
4. It gives you wisdom for living.

### How can you 'feed' on it?
There are different types of food that are good for us and we eat them in different ways. We would pick up an apple, but we'd use a knife and fork to eat a steak. So we feed on the Word of God in various ways.

It is important to recognise the different types of literature in the Bible. For example the Psalms are poetic songs whereas the Gospels are mainly narratives (describing events).

### Ways to feed on the Word of God:
1. Set a good time for you to read the Bible each day. For some people the morning is best, for others it could be late evening. Set a time that works for you.
2. Before you start, pray and ask God to speak to you from his

Word, and for the Holy Spirit to guide you.

3. Read short portions on a daily basis. Begin with a Gospel, then maybe Acts, then other parts of the New Testament. Read some of the Old Testament, like Genesis, to get a better idea of the whole context. Read a Psalm every so often as they really help us express ourselves to God as the Psalmist did, often expressing frustration or other emotions.

4. Write down verses that seem to speak to you. Think about them; ask questions about what they mean. Ponder and chew over a few words that are meaningful to you and let them sink deep into your heart.

5. Put into practice what you hear the Word saying to you.

6. Read and study the Bible with other believers too.

7. Get some study aids, like a Study Bible or use websites like www.searchgodsword.org and study the Bible a bit deeper, getting an understanding of the context and what it means.

If you develop a good and regular practice of reading the Bible it will become a rich resource to you throughout your life.

> *"I have made reading the Word of God a very regular practice in my life. Sometimes I'll read a lot, at other times just focus on one verse a day for a few weeks. I don't get legalistic about it but do find being disciplined helps. Some days it doesn't seem to say much but on occasions it's as if a verse or a word leaps off the page to me. At other times in my life, the Holy Spirit has brought a Bible reference into my mind which, when I have looked it up it has been just what I needed to hear or the answer to some question I've been pondering. Getting to know the Word of God has been one of the key factors in my growth as a disciple of Jesus."*

## Have a Look

What does 2 Timothy 3:16-17 say about the value of Scripture? List the things it says it is useful for:

...................................................................................................

...................................................................................................

...................................................................................................

...................................................................................................

Look up Psalm 119:105. How does this verse describe God's Word? What might this look like in your life?

...................................................................................................

...................................................................................................

...................................................................................................

...................................................................................................

## Practical Response: Bible Reading

Write down or get hold of a plan for reading other parts of the Bible over the next few months. Then plan how you might read from the Bible over the months after that.

## Questions for Reflection:

1.Why do you think it is important to read from the Bible regularly?

2. What might help you to better understand the meaning of different books of the Bible?

3. In what you have read of the Bible so far, how has it helped you in your life?

\*\*\*\*\*\*\*\*\*\*

### Growth Point:

Start to learn a verse from the Bible off by heart every so often.

Make this a practice for the rest of your life.

\*\*\*\*\*\*\*\*\*\*

# 14. Hearing the Voice of God

*The Secret Place*

*"Blessed is the man who listens to me, Watching daily at my doors,*
*Waiting at my doorway."*
*- Hebrew Proverb*

Does God really speak to us? Is it possible for you to actually hear God and if so, then how does he speak? How can you know that it is God's voice and not just your imagination?

Throughout the pages of the Bible we find lots of people encountering God in different ways and hearing him speak to them. This happened in Jesus life, but it wasn't just the 'big names' like Moses and Mary who heard God speak, but also some very ordinary people.

## Why does God speak to us?
He speaks to us because we are in a relationship with him, because he loves and likes us. He speaks to us to guide us about specific situations, to warn us, to reassure us, to encourage us and to reveal things that he wants us to partner in with him.

## How does God speak to us?
He communicates with us in lots of different ways – he is very creative! Here's a list of some of the ways - but never limit God!

## 1. Through the Bible

This is a most common way and anything else we sense God saying to us should never go against what the Bible says. The Bible tells me to love my wife, so if I have a dream telling me not to love my wife, then that is clearly not from God.

## 2. Through dreams

We do all dream despite some folks saying they never do – they just don't remember them. Not all our dreams are from God, in fact probably only a few. Most of the time it is just our mind sorting out stuff that happened during that day. But at times God will communicate through a dream. Such a dream usually appears to us very vividly. Write down such dreams and ask God if he is speaking to you in this. Ask him what it means, especially any symbolism in it.

## 3. Through visions and mental pictures

God is very visual, and he communicates a lot in pictures. A vision can be like a dream except you're awake! Visions will often have symbolic stuff in them but sometimes are very clear.

## 4. Through creation and life's events

God can draw our attention to natural things and 'speak' to us through these. Many of Jesus' parables drew lessons from nature. God also speaks to us through the events that happen in our lives. God is always speaking and it's really a question of who is listening.

## 5. Through angels

Angels are God's messengers. At times people may encounter an angel who brings a message from God to them. This happened a good number of times in the Bible and still does today.

**6. God's still small voice.** God speaking to us is always special but not always spectacular. Often it is like an inner whisper but we just sense this is not our own thoughts.

### How do we know it's God?

You don't, so you have to test it. Does it line up with the truth in the Bible? Does it fit with what you know of Jesus and does it honour him? Do you sense this is something different? Does it produce good fruit?

Some years ago when I was leading a small church in Glasgow, I sensed God's voice very clearly speak to me during the night about our church's financial situation. I spoke to others in the leadership about this and they recognised this word to be from God. We shared this with the church and acted on it. The fruit was that within no time at all, our church had a tremendous financial breakthrough.

God doesn't always speak so clearly; often it is in more obscure ways. Why is this? So that we spend time with him, asking him about it and seeking his wisdom. He likes us to spend time with him.

### Who does God speak to in these ways?

People sometimes think it is just the very special or spiritual people God speaks to like this. However we are all special to him. God speaks to those who are listening. In fact Jesus said that God has hidden things from the wise and learned, and revealed them to little children. It is when we come to God like little, trusting children that he speaks most.

> *"When I was a teenager I heard a man who had been a missionary in Africa speaking one night. At that age I usually got bored listening to speakers but I remember things he said to this day. He told the story of one night when he was in his small hut in the village he was staying in at that time. It was during a period of civil war in that country. He was lying on his bed when he sensed the voice of God tell him to get under the bed and lie still. He didn't understand why but obeyed what he sensed God was saying to him. Moments later a hail of bullets cut through the wall just above his bed as a jeep with rebel soldiers drove through the village. Had he not heard and obeyed the voice of God he would have been killed that very night"*

## Have a Look

Look up these verses and see in what ways God spoke to people:

Matthew 1:20.........................................................................................

Acts 18:9-10.........................................................................................

1 Kings 19:12-13.........................................................................................

## Practical Response: Show up and Shut up

Set aside 5 minutes a day this week to sit silently and just listen to God. Look on this as an appointment with God. At first you may get distracted and your thoughts wander all over the place. That's OK, persevere and see what happens.

**Questions for Reflection:**

1. For what purposes would God speak to us throughout our lives?
2. Have you ever been aware of God speaking to you in some manner? What did he say?
3. How might you develop listening to God? What would help you to do this?

**\*\*\*\*\*\*\*\*\*\***

### Growth Point:

Be quick to listen and slow to speak (that's good advice from the letter of James chapter 1v19).

**\*\*\*\*\*\*\*\*\*\***

## Part 5 – Living in Community
### *Introduction*

The previous sections of this manual have dealt mainly with your relationship with God and how that works out in your life. This section will consider your relationship with other followers of Jesus. We are not called to be on our own, but to live in community and relationship with other believers.

A good amount of Jesus' teaching, as well as a large portion of the New Testament letters, deal with relating to each other. It is only in relationships that we can fully understand the life and love of God; and it is only through relationships with people that we can fully show the love of God.

This area of relationships and community is also where most tensions and problems arise for us. Jesus is easy to get on with and so are some people, but others aren't! We are all different and view life from differing standpoints. We don't always agree with each other, and some people do things that annoy and irritate us. Rather than seeing this as all bad, it is good to realise that it is a challenge of life, and to learn to appreciate the great variety with which God has made us.

In this section we will explain what 'church' really is, hopefully dispelling some of the common misunderstandings, and see how we can grow in healthy, life-enhancing relationships.

## 15. What is the point of Church?

*Living in Community*

*" Let us not give up meeting together ... but let us encourage one another."*
*– Author of Hebrews*

Once when on a holiday Helen and I got chatting to an older couple at breakfast. They asked if we liked churches. We replied that we did and in fact that I was a leader of one. They got a little embarrassed and back tracked saying they were only interested in the old buildings, not what went on inside them!

### What is the church and what is it not?

There are a lot of popular misconceptions about the church, often people thinking it to be a particular building. The early church met in homes and other places rather than in 'sacred' buildings. A church is a group or community of believers who are called together by God to encourage one another and to live out Jesus Christ's mission together. The Bible speaks of the church as the Body of Christ with Jesus as the head, as the Bride of Christ and as a family of believers or people of God. The church is not somewhere we go to but a group of fellow believers we belong to.

The church is not a club or a holy huddle, but it is a group that exists ultimately for the benefit of those who are not yet part of it.

**Why are there different types of churches with various names?**

In God's eyes we are all the one big family of believers in Jesus. But because we see things and interpret things differently, there have arisen many types of churches and various denominations or groupings of churches. This is not necessarily a bad thing, though sometimes it came out of dispute. In fact it can be quite healthy if we can appreciate the good in the various expressions of church life, learning from and valuing each other. Having many types of churches means there is more likely to be a suitable church for the many different types of people around. It is also good to know that we are part of one expression of church among many millions throughout the earth.

**Why is it important to meet together?**

We all need encouragement and the strength we get from one another. Only through meaningful relationships can we work out much of what God tells us to do. If we don't meet together, we often will struggle with discouragement and a feeling of isolation. It is actually when we are really struggling or feeling bad about ourselves that it is most important to meet with others instead of being tempted to withdraw.

**What do we do when we get together?**

While the format and style of what goes on at church gatherings will vary from church to church, there are some common elements.

1. **Praise.** We come together to praise God and thank him for his goodness. We often do a good bit of this through singing

songs or hymns. There is something quite special about the power of song.

2.  **Prayer.** It is a time to pray together, and there is power in us agreeing together in prayer. We also can pray for each other for our various needs, for healing and so forth.

3.  **Teaching.** It is time to receive teaching from God's Word which helps us understand the Bible better, see things that we maybe wouldn't have noticed, and get instruction on how to apply the Word in our lives.

4.  **Giving.** We will usually take up a collection of money, also called the offering, so we have the opportunity to bring our gifts to God together where they can be used in meaningful ways for God's Kingdom work.

Some churches will have a strong emphasis on healing and miracles, others on a set liturgy of worship; some will have choirs and some will have different types of music. What really matters is that we encounter God together in these times; that we are built up in our faith, and go back into our world more equipped to make Jesus known.

*"Having been in various churches over the years, what belonging to church means to me is having a safe place to come together with other Christians to worship God, in complete freedom from 'rules' and the expectations of others. I come to church to thank God in my worship offered to him; to be built up as he ministers to me through music and his Word unpacked and applied to real life. Church helps me grow in confidence, in the knowledge that Christ is making me into who I am meant to be, through relating to God and the supportive friendship of those on this journey of faith. Then, taking what I learn, to use as I live out my life, I desire that other people would come into an understanding of who Jesus is, and what he can do in their lives"*

## Have a Look

Look up Philippians 2:1-4. Write down from this passage the things that make for good relationships and the things to avoid:

..................................................................................................

..................................................................................................

..................................................................................................

..................................................................................................

..................................................................................................

..................................................................................................

..................................................................................................

## Practical Response: Be in Community

Commit yourself to be part of a local group of believers and to participate in the life of that community. Write down some ways you think you could contribute to the group.

..................................................................................................
..................................................................................................
..................................................................................................
..................................................................................................
..................................................................................................

## Questions for Reflection:

1. Why is it important to be part of a church?
2. What benefits are there in meeting together with other believers?
3. What might make you feel more of a part of your local church?

\*\*\*\*\*\*\*\*\*\*

## Growth Point:

It is helpful for you to be committed to one local church, but at the same time it is good to develop a respect for other churches that maybe do something a bit different from yours. On appropriate occasions join in events that embrace the wider church.

\*\*\*\*\*\*\*\*\*\*

# 16. Having Purposeful Relationships

*Living in Community*

*"From him (Jesus) the whole body, joined and held together by every supporting ligament, grows and builds itself up in love, as each part does its work."*
*– Paul the Apostle*

Spending time with some good friends, just chatting, drinking coffee and doing nothing much can be very pleasant for a time. But relationships are meant to have a purpose outside of themselves. The church needs to be a community with an outlet that gives and goes into the world. The reason the Dead Sea in Israel is 'dead' is because it has no outlet; nothing flows from it, only into it. Because of this fact, that body of water cannot sustain life.

## Fellowship

A term that is often used in churches is 'fellowship.' However it is often used without any real sense of its meaning. The word comes from the New Testament and has the sense of sharing in a common purpose together. Jesus calls us to follow him and to do this together. He sent his disciples out to heal the sick and proclaim the good news, and he always sent them in two's, not on their own.

Jesus brings us into relationship with himself (and the Father and Holy Spirit), he also brings us into relationship with other believers, but the full experience of these relationships will only come when we move in purpose together. We grow in relationships with others as we do things with them.

## Life enhancing relationships

In life we can be involved in lots of relationships, some of which are very rewarding and others may be quite draining. Relationships don't tend to just happen; they need to be developed and worked at. It is important to build and develop relationships that are life enhancing to both parties. In these sorts of relationships we add value to each other and increase the effectiveness of each other's lives.

## How the church is built

The church needs to be built on life enhancing relationships. God sets in place certain people with particular gifts and functions to equip and enable the church community to grow. The Bible uses the terms apostle, prophet, evangelist, pastor and teacher to describe these people. So what do these terms mean and what do these people do?

**An apostle** is someone who is sent to establish new works and new leaders.

**A prophet** is someone who regularly brings revelations from God to inspire, encourage and strengthen the church.

**An evangelist** is someone who draws many people to Jesus and trains others to do so too.

**A pastor** is like a shepherd who cares for the church flock, guiding and protecting the people.

**A teacher** is one who trains God's people in the truths of the Word of God, and teaches them how to feed themselves.

These five functions are all designed to equip God's people to do their own works for the Lord, and to build the church in faith, knowledge and maturity in Christ.

### Good leadership

The church needs good leadership in order to develop well and rise up into its potential in God's purposes. Good leadership is never manipulative or controlling. Instead good leaders lead by example, serve the church, and release people to become all they can be in God's grace.

In the various styles of churches today, all sorts of terms are used for the local leaders, such as minister, pastor, vicar, elder, or simply leader. No matter what term is used, it should never be about position (which can lead to pride), but about serving and loving the church.

The great truth about being part of this body of Christ is that every part is needed, and every part has a role to play. No-one is to be a mere spectator. We are all on the team together and we all get to play a part in the great purposes of God for his church, and through his church into the world.

> *"When my husband and I first started to go along to Church to have a look and see what it was all about, there were one or two women who befriended me. Our children were similar ages and as new Mums we had something in common. What started as a 'Hello! How are you?' chat on Sunday morning 9 years ago, developed into two of my deepest and strongest of friendships.*
>
> *The women suggested we might meet once a week for a catch up and prayer time. We always talked a lot, drank coffee and prayed for each other's needs. We sometimes looked at the Bible, or we talked about a book we had agreed to read together. I can't tell you just how special this time was. As we met, our friendship grew incredibly, we shared our highs and lows, and God answered many prayers throughout that time. As years passed, our families grew up together and our friendship deepened – our families became close, supporting each other in many ways.*
>
> *Over time, God also used us to befriend others, provide meals for the sick and in need in our community and support others; both practically and with prayer. I can say with my hand on my heart that I would not be where I am today without this relationship and am so much the richer for it"* - Moira

**Have a Look**

Read Acts 2:42-47 and write down what you see there about relationships and purpose in the early church.

...................................................................................

...................................................................................

...................................................................................

...................................................................................

...................................................................................

...................................................................................

...................................................................................

**Practical Response: Build Relationships**

Think about what relationships you need to develop and with whom that would be life enhancing for you and them. Aim to do some things to build such relationships.

**Questions for Reflection:**

1. What do you think are the main ingredients of good relationships?

2. What do you see as the purposes God has for your life?

3. How would any of those purposes be better worked out in relationship with other people?

*********

**Growth Point:**

Get into the way of praying with other people. Don't be afraid of hearing your own voice – it really helps to pray out loud.

*********

# 17. It's all about Love

*Living in Community*

*" This is my command: love each other"*
*– Jesus*

The great commandments in the New Testament, which really sum up the Christian life, are to love the Lord with everything you are and have, and to love each other, loving your neighbour as you love yourself.

God is love; he doesn't just show love, it is the essential nature of who he is. We can love because he first loved us. He has shown us what this true love is, demonstrating this by sending his Son Jesus to die in our place. The truth that God loves you unconditionally shows that you are lovable. Knowing you are loved and lovable frees you to love others. Only as you know and grow in God's love will you be freed from the fears and anxieties that keep you from giving of yourself and loving others. The key to making church work and to making relationships fruitful is that we love each other the same unconditional way that God loves us.

**Love one another – John 13:34; Romans 13:8; 1 John 3:11**
So what does that look like? The New Testament gives a list of 'one another' commands that are practical expressions of this love.

**Be devoted to one another – Romans 12:10:** This term means loving affection, and describes the mutual love between parents and children, and between husbands and wives.

**Honour one another – Romans 12:10:** This means to give high value to others and to give preference to their needs and feelings.

**Live in harmony with one another – Romans 12:16:** The idea here is to be of the same mind, as we all have our minds fixed on Jesus and what he wants.

**Accept one another – Romans 15:7:** To accept means to take to oneself, to receive into your own home. It is opposite to judging one another.

**Serve one another – Galatians 5:13:** Jesus demonstrated true service, he came to serve, and serving others is a sign of true greatness in his estimation.

**Carry each other's burdens – Galatians 6:2:** This means to help each other, sharing the load of anyone else's troubles and struggles. It is giving a helping hand to those who need it.

**Encourage one another daily – Hebrews 3:13:** We all need encouragement and it is also easy to give. A simple word, compliment, or even smile can make a big difference.

**Be humble towards one another – 1 Peter 5:5:** In all of the above, true humility is vital. If we have an over-inflated opinion of ourselves we won't treat others well. If we have too low an opinion of ourselves, we will probably be too shy or afraid to show much love. We need to know God's opinion of us which leads to a true humility.

It is great to belong to a family of people who love each other, and have each other's interests at heart. But this love for each other does more than that. It is the best demonstration to the world that we are Jesus' disciples and it is the greatest attraction to draw others to Jesus himself. Jesus said so very plainly: *"A new command I give you: Love one another. As I have loved you, so you must love one another. By this everyone will know that you are my disciples, if you love one another."* (John 13:34-35)

---

*"As I've travelled to various places and countries, it has been wonderful to find other followers of Jesus from different cultures, and to find a love for each other due to our common bond in Jesus Christ. This love has not been just talk, but has been shown in hospitality, encouragements, and others practical ways. To meet people who look and talk quite unlike yourself, and to immediately feel you belong with them and are part of one family as brothers and sisters is quite amazing."*

---

**Have a Look**

Look up some of the other 'one another' commands and see what they tell us about how we can relate well to each other:

Romans 15:14 ...................................................................................

Ephesians 4:32 ........................................................................

Ephesians 5:19 ........................................................................

Colossians 3:16 ........................................................................

Hebrews 10:24 ........................................................................

James 5:16 ........................................................................

## Practical Response: Showing Love

Think who you could express one of these commands to this week.
For example, who could you encourage and how would you do that?
Or who might you serve and in what ways?

........................................................................
........................................................................
........................................................................
........................................................................
........................................................................

## Questions for Reflection:

1. Why is it important to first know God's love for us in order for us
to love other people well?

2. What hinders you in any way from showing love to others? How
could you overcome these hindrances?

3. In what practical ways have you received love from others? What
did this mean to you?

**\*\*\*\*\*\*\*\*\*\***

## Growth Point:

Invite someone out for coffee and encourage them, or practice hospitality by inviting someone or some people for a meal at your house.

**\*\*\*\*\*\*\*\*\*\***

# 18. Unoffendable

## Living in Community

*"An offended brother is more unyielding than a fortified city"*
– Hebrew Proverb

Have you ever taken the huff over something someone said to you, or if you were overlooked or ignored? If your answer is 'no' then you are an exception!

An offended heart is very hard to reach out to, and it is the taking of offence that is one of the biggest causes of relationships breaking down. Offence is like a brick wall we put round our heart. It is also therefore one of the biggest causes of people falling away from following Jesus and from being part of their Christian community. It is really important that we do not give in to offence but seek to develop an unoffendable heart.

### Who do we get offended by?

We don't tend to be offended by the words and reactions of strangers or people who have little significance in our lives. We are more likely to get offended by people close to us. We can even feel offended by God, for example if we feel he hasn't answered our prayers. It is those who are significant to us that are the most likely to cause us offence.

### What can cause us to be offended?

When we have an expectation to be loved and accepted and when we perceive that that doesn't happen, we can feel offence. We can get offended when we feel we are not valued or respected or taken seriously. When we feel that we've been ignored, overlooked or dismissed we can take offence, or if we feel insulted or put down. Sometimes we can take offence when absolutely no offence was intended.

**Why do we take offence?**

Offence may be given but you don't have to take it! When we do take offence it is usually being built on previous wounds, fears and insecurities in our lives. For example, if someone suffered a lot of ridicule as a child which hurt them deeply, then even if someone says something to them as a joke but it sounds like ridicule, then they may well take great offence as it strikes on the open wound in their life. Ultimately it is our sense of pride that gets offended, and pride is the main thing the Lord wants to remove from our lives.

If your sense of personal value and significance is rooted anywhere else other than in your relationship with Jesus, then you will suffer offence at times.

**How can we become unoffendable?**

You will get hurt at times, or ignored or overlooked but you don't have to give in to offence at these times. If you see that Jesus gives you extreme personal value and significance, and you are secure in him, then no-one can take that from you. No remark, rebuff or rejection from people can alter the truth of who you are in Christ Jesus.

**Keeping an unoffendable heart:**

1. Let go of any sense of pride in yourself.

2. Embrace your new self which is secure in Christ, in the acceptance, approval, affirmation and adequacy that he gives to you.

3. When any offensive remarks or actions come your way, refuse to take offence or get caught up in it.

4. Live continually in an attitude of forgiveness towards anyone who wrongs you in any way.

*"For years Tom felt like he was always being criticised and could never do anything quite right. He would get made a fool of in school because he was useless at sports. His class results never seemed good enough for his father's liking. When he became a Christian he felt he had a new life and a new start. But then when anyone said anything that remotely sounded like criticism he would react badly. Tom began to realise that he was still letting the old Tom react to people and that this wasn't the real him any longer. He chose to forgive those who had mocked him when he was young and live in the truth that God loved him, valued and approved of him just as he was. He soon found that he no longer reacted to the slightest negative comment but was able to take himself less seriously and enjoy the truth that God still loved him even when he did mess up."*

**Have a Look**

Look up 1 Corinthians 13:4-7 and write down what these verses say to you about being offended or wronged:

.......................................................................................................
.......................................................................................................
.......................................................................................................
.......................................................................................................
.......................................................................................................
.......................................................................................................
.......................................................................................................

**Practical Response: Being Unoffendable**

Ask God to heal and remove any roots of offence from your life. Put the four steps on the previous page into practice in your life this week.

**Questions for Reflection:**

1. Do you tend to react badly to being criticised or ignored? If so, why do you think this is?
2. Do you take yourself too seriously or can you laugh at yourself?
3. In what or in whom is your sense of personal value rooted?

\*\*\*\*\*\*\*\*\*\*

**Growth Point:**

Learn to laugh more in life, especially at yourself.

\*\*\*\*\*\*\*\*\*\*

## Part 6 – Advancing the Kingdom

*Introduction*

*"Our Father in heaven, hallowed be your name, your Kingdom come, your will be done..."* – Jesus

As Jesus went about his life he was constantly teaching others about the Kingdom of God. Not only this, he was demonstrating signs of the Kingdom through the healings, miracles and transformations that took place through him. It was not only about talk but power.

The Kingdom of God could be defined as the rule and reign of God, rather than a geographical place. Seeing a Kingdom advance is about a King's domain increasing. That is what we want to see happening here on earth. It is not only something we look forward to in heaven but we can see signs of the Kingdom in the here and now. Jesus taught us to pray: "Your Kingdom come, your will be done, on earth as it is in heaven". God's desire is to bring the atmosphere of heaven down here. He wants us to partner with him in that.

Jesus said he was the light of the world. However in Matthew 5, he tells us that we are also the light of the world. He passed the job of advancing the Kingdom onto us. We have to be agents of transformation, telling others about the Kingdom and bringing about its signs. "The Kingdom of God is at hand" (Mark 1:15). That means it is within reach for us to bring it down!

# 19. Walking in your Authority

*Advancing the Kingdom*

*"All authority in heaven and earth has been given to me" – Jesus*

To understand more about our authority, we need to take it right back to the beginning and look at God's original plan. He created Adam and Eve to rule over creation as his representatives: "The Lord took the man and put him in the Garden of Eden to work it and take care of it" (Genesis 2:15). His original intention was for us to have authority here on earth.

But as a result of man's sin, we relinquished our God-given right to authority and allowed the enemy the right to rule. However, this was about to change. After centuries of waiting for Jesus, the promised rescuer to come on the scene, he arrived. He conquered sin and defeated death, becoming the one Satan had no authority over, and as a result, he regained what was lost at the beginning in the Garden of Eden.

Satan knew this is why Jesus came. He tried to hold onto his authority by offering Jesus it at the time of his baptism in the desert. "All of this I will give you if you bow down and worship me" (story found in Luke 4:1-13). However, Jesus knew it could only be truly recaptured if death was overcome. What is even more incredible though is that, rather than God seeing how we messed up at the beginning, he said, 'I am giving the authority back to you, the church. It's time for you to rule and reign with me again.'

What does that mean? It means you and I have the unrestrained right, and we have the permission to release his power in the here and now. Our purpose is to demonstrate the Kingdom, to bring about heaven's agenda on earth and to have dominion over the works of the enemy. These works may take the form of sickness, injustice, or even broken lives. The enemy does not want us to know this truth because if we do, then his power here on earth will diminish. Through our words and through prayer we may have more of a say of what goes on here than maybe we are led to believe.

### How do I get it?
Just as the disciples received authority to heal the sick and to drive out darkness, it has also been given to us. We do not need to earn our way to receiving it. It is dependent only on our position as his sons and daughters. We do not need to wait until that moment he "officially" commissions us; he already has when we gave our lives to him. However, we will only bring about transformation to lives and to this world as we choose to remain in him. With the realisation that God has given us authority, we must exercise it or else it is of no use. Police officers are given authority by the government that they serve. If they didn't employ it, then there would be even higher levels of crime. Authority must require an act; otherwise it will not create change.

### Walking in it
As you begin to release God's Kingdom through your life, the following are some keys to help you on your way:

1. Each morning, ask God to fill you with his Holy Spirit afresh.

2. "Make the most of every opportunity" (Ephesians 5:16). Ask God to help you realise opportunities in your day. It could be in your workplace, with family or out shopping. You may simply pray for someone or encourage them.

3. "Pray without ceasing" (1 Thessalonians 5:17). This verse does not mean being locked away in your bedroom praying 24/7. It is about being in constant conversation with the Father and listening to what he may be saying to you.

4. Learn from others who do it. Start off by reading the gospels and see how Jesus did it. He is the best example to follow. I want him to be my standard. Alongside this, it may be useful to read some books from experienced individuals or you could attend a training course. Only do this though if you plan on doing something with it!

5. Get connected with others already doing it and join them. Jesus often sent his disciples out in pairs. We get greater boldness, support and encouragement this way.

6. Give it a go. You really only learn from trying. If you mess up then God will pick you up and let you have as many shots as you need.

> *"For a many years in my Christian Faith, I seemed to be waiting for God to release me into the things he had for me. I was waiting for my commissioning into doing the ministry that Jesus did here on Earth. I had heard people talk about being part of praying for people, healing the sick, sharing Jesus in a real way and I thought that I wanted to do those things, however I was waiting. In hindsight, I don't know what I was waiting for; maybe the audible voice of God, an angel to appear in my room, or a conference speaker telling me that now was my time. These things didn't happen, however I came to the revelation that everything in the Bible tells me that now is my time. Now is my time to bring light to the darkness. Jesus already has commissioned me; he did that when I gave my life to him. I don't need to wait for my moment, because it's already here. Since then I have begun to step out in things and have seen many more people touched by God through my life and it makes me feel even more alive!"* - Colin

**Have a Look**

Look up the following verses and write down what you see about your authority:

*Luke 10:19* ......................................................................

......................................................................

......................................................................

......................................................................

*Mark 13:34* .....................................................................
.....................................................................
.....................................................................
.....................................................................

*John 15:5* .....................................................................
.....................................................................
.....................................................................
.....................................................................

**Practical Response:**

Take some time to think about what you are doing with your day tomorrow. Ask God to reveal the opportunities you have to release his Kingdom. When something comes to mind, ask him to help you bring it about.

**Questions for Reflection:**

1. What do you now realise you have the authority to do? What does it really mean?
2. What would you like to see happen through your life as a result of the authority God has given to you? How do you plan to use it?
3. How can you build time into your day so that you "remain in him"?

\*\*\*\*\*\*\*\*\*

## Growth Point:

Take some time to find a training course or conference that will equip you even further to release the good works of the Kingdom. Ask your church leaders or friends to recommend somewhere. It could be a day conference, weekend away or even a week in the summer.

\*\*\*\*\*\*\*\*\*

# 20. Kingdom Invasion: Your Role

*Advancing the Kingdom*

*"I chose you and put you into the world to bear fruit"*
*– Jesus*

If we forget about our true identity we can lose sight of our purpose. We may feel like others are more qualified or more gifted than us to advance the Kingdom. We can feel like we have nothing to give, but when we look at the truth of what God says, we see that we have a part to play.

## Ordinary doing the Extraordinary

Jesus went against the grain of culture in the selection of the twelve disciples. Rabbis (Jewish spiritual leaders) at the time chose disciples or students that had a very high degree of education and knew the Old Testament inside out. The aim of a Rabbi was to find those who had the potential to follow in their footsteps. However Jesus did not choose his disciples based on intellect or natural ability. Included in the twelve were fishermen, a tax collector and a political enthusiast. When we look at them they were just ordinary men. There was nothing special about them, however Jesus changed that all around. They became a force that forever changed the world and showed others what could happen when you followed God. We sometimes talk about having faith in Jesus but we rarely mention that he has faith in us. That is why he chose us. He believes that through him we have what it takes to be someone that can be part of advancing the Kingdom of God.

## Your part

Your role in this is just as important as anyone else's. No one's is more significant or less valuable. For the church to be fully effective and to have maximum impact in this world, everyone must play their part. In 1 Corinthians 12, Paul draws parallels between the church and the human body. They are both made up of many pieces but are all one unit. Every part relies on another, those seen and unseen. For the Kingdom to be advanced we need one another. As an individual, you cannot share the gospel everywhere in this world or bring about transformation to every single person's life. Though this sounds like an exciting challenge, I do not think God has this planned for us. He wants us to come together and for each to pick up their part. As we do this we will see communities and nations turn to God. Our framework is seeing the Kingdom of God advance and bringing about heaven on earth. We must discover what excites us about this and pursue it. God has maybe placed dreams and desires inside of us that we would love to see happen. We can't do everything, but we can do our bit.

## Shaping Culture

Twelve ordinary men became part of a group that changed so many lives and communities. Through them whole households were transformed – men and women, young and old, slaves and free people. This transforming power spread like wildfire through the

Roman Empire and beyond. Could it be that God is calling you to be part of a force that continues that impact? Where you see people everyday being touched by the love of God? Where you pray for someone's transformation and it happens? Where you see our society shaped by God's values again? This is God's invitation. The realms of education, medicine, entertainment, politics and business are just some of the areas that shape how the world lives and thinks. He is looking for people to invade all sectors of culture so that change can take place. You don't need to go somewhere to do it; you can start with where you are.

---

*"I grew up believing that people like me were insignificant. I was never given the freedom to dream that I might have a God-given destiny. God began to poke around at roots of shyness, fear, even apathy, getting me to a point of wanting those negative attributes to disappear from my life forever, with a call to work in God's Kingdom. It was still hard to conceive that God had a 'world-changing' destiny for me; but a train of events and people invading my life changed all that, and the seed of belief that I just MIGHT have a role to play in seeing God's Kingdom come, began to grow. Since those days, in the early '80's, that seed has grown into a driving passion and opportunities to see God offer salvation, perform miracles, heal, and set people free in many nations. From the parochial, fear-centred teen/twenty something, with no desire to speak to, or pray for others, it has been a journey that has blown my mind over 30 years now. God uses the weak and the foolish — I'm so glad he does!" - Peter*

**Have a Look**

Look up the story of Jesus calling Simon Peter and his brother Andrew in Matthew 4:18-22. How would these two brothers have felt when Jesus called them to follow him?

...........................................................................................

...........................................................................................

...........................................................................................

Why did they immediately drop what they were doing?

...........................................................................................

...........................................................................................

...........................................................................................

How would their father have felt?

...........................................................................................

...........................................................................................

...........................................................................................

**Practical Response:**

Spend some time in prayer. Ask God to reveal to you what you can do practically to see the Kingdom of God advance in your home, workplace or even community. Write this down and over the coming days and weeks act on it.

**Questions for Reflection:**

1. How does it make you feel that God believes you have what it takes to be part of advancing his Kingdom?
2. Are there any dreams or desires that you feel God has given you? Is there anything that really excites you and you want to see

happen?

3. What would the Kingdom of God look like in your community?

\*\*\*\*\*\*\*\*\*

## Growth Point:

Sometimes people can feel underappreciated in what they do. Become or continue to be a person that encourages. This could be someone in church or at work. Make them feel valued and thank them for what they bring to the place.

\*\*\*\*\*\*\*\*\*

## 21. The Miraculous is for Today

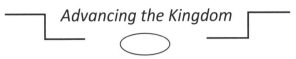

*Advancing the Kingdom*

*"Very truly I tell you, whoever believes in me will do the works I have been doing, and they will do even greater things than these, because I am going to the Father"*
*– Jesus*

Throughout the gospels we see Jesus performing many miracles. These include the multiplication of food, raising of the dead, bringing sight to the blind and turning water into wine. Being able to do the latter would make us very popular guests at any party! Jesus was not able to do these things because he was God - he gave up his own divine power when he came to earth. Jesus said himself, "The Son can do nothing." These wonders happened because he was full of the Holy Spirit and at one with his Father. He was showing what could happen when someone fully grasped their identity and authority in God.

 In Scripture we see that miraculous acts didn't disappear when Jesus went to be with the Father. "Everyone was filled with awe, and many wonders and miraculous signs were done by the apostles" (Acts 2:43). Throughout the book of Acts we see several demonstrations of God's power through his followers. As the apostles went preaching about the Kingdom from place to place, signs and wonders followed them. As a result, it pointed people in the direction of God because it caught their attention and they were able to see the power for themselves. Many came to faith through these times and, on occasions, thousands were impacted. When you see the impossible happen in a situation, it cuts across doubts and arguments.

## Miracles Today

"Go to the lost...Tell them that the Kingdom is here. Bring health to the sick. Raise the dead. Touch the untouchables. Kick out demons" (Matthew 10:7-8, The Message). This was Jesus' call to the disciples and his call to us today. Seeing the miraculous happen is supposed to be part of the normal Christian life. It is not something reserved for worship leaders, church leaders or conference speakers. It is a call for us all. Across the world, Christians are seeing the miraculous of God come about in, and through, their lives. We may not hear these stories through the media, but they are happening. Illnesses likes cancer and depression are being healed; there are testimonies of miraculous protection in dangerous areas, and supernatural provision of finance and resources. This is just the start of them. We may not have seen the miraculous through our own lives and churches yet; however we must believe what Jesus says. We can't base our beliefs on what we have experienced. It must come from Scripture. Jesus said whoever believes in me will do the works I have, and even greater. Do you want this in your life?

## Healing the Sick

One way we can begin to see the miraculous happen through our lives is by praying for others. If someone is suffering from sickness or disease, it is God's heart to heal and we are his hands and feet on earth. The Bible records a variety of healings and means of healing. This emphasises yet again that the Christian life is based on relationship with God rather than techniques. As a starter, listed below are some simple steps that can help you pray for someone:

1. **Ask** – What does this person need prayer for? If it is for pain or sickness, ask them about it so that you can effectively pray for it.

2. **Inform** – Let the person know what you are going to do. You may lay a hand on them (Mark 6:5), but if you are going to do this, ask their permission. You want the individual to feel comfortable and prepared.

3. **Pray** – It doesn't have to be long-winded. Keep it simple. Invite God to show his love to the person and to touch their need. For healing, speak to the illness and pain and tell it to be gone. Ask for strength and wholeness to come.

4. **See what God does** – Don't be afraid to ask what individuals are feeling. God may be speaking to them or they may be experiencing him. If the pain can be measured, ask them if there is any change. Thank God for what he is doing and pray for more.

5. **Encourage** – As you finish, let them know what God thinks about them. Encourage them. They may have felt nothing; however tell the individual about God's heart for them. If they have experienced something, let them know that it is God at work in them.

Remember, these are supposed to be signs that point people to Jesus.

> *"I used to read scripture and really just dream about seeing healing and miracles happen through my life. I asked God if he could use me in this way. After a long time of praying for it to happen, I finally realised the miraculous would only come if I stepped out and did something about it. Despite still feeling inadequate and fearful, over the past few years I have really begun to start to pray with individuals outside of the church. I have now prayed with, and for, lots of folk especially for healing. As a result, I have seen and heard about God transforming lives through these times of prayer. God has taken away depression. Back pain has been healed. Migraines have gone. Tumours have shrunk. Blocked organs have been opened. Swelling in legs has disappeared. These are just some of the examples. Our God is the God of the impossible and he chooses us to bring it about. I am just an ordinary young guy but God still uses me. If he can use me, he can use you. There have been times as well where I have seen no immediate difference in someone's life; however no one I have ever prayed for has ever left without feeling a sense of his peace and love."*

## Have a Look

Look up the following verses and write down what you see happen through the Apostles:

*Acts 3:1-10* .................................................................................

.................................................................................

*Acts 9:36-43* ............................................................

...................................................................

...................................................................

...................................................................

*Acts 28:1-10* ...........................................................

...................................................................

...................................................................

...................................................................

## Practical Response: Boldness

Read Acts 4:29-31. For the miraculous to happen we need greater boldness in our lives. Take some time with God and let him give that to you. Ask him to remove any fear or feelings of inadequacy. Let his truth be spoken over you. During this week, step out and pray with someone who is in pain or is sick.

## Questions for Reflection:

1. What difference would seeing more miraculous signs and wonders have on your friends, family and community?
2. Have you or anyone you know ever experienced a miracle? If so, what happened?
3. What would stop you from praying for someone? What do you need God to do for you?

\*\*\*\*\*\*\*\*\*\*

**Growth Point:**

All the time we are coming across people who do not feel 100%.
Rather than give sympathy to the person, offer to pray for them.
The only thing they have to lose is their pain or sickness. To be part
of the miraculous, you must move out of your comfort zone.

\*\*\*\*\*\*\*\*\*\*

# 22. Looking after the Poor

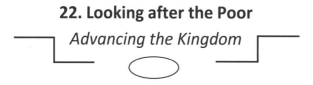

*Advancing the Kingdom*

*"He who is gracious to a poor man lends to the Lord, and he will repay him for his good deed"*
*– Hebrew Proverb*

Alongside the miraculous being part of our lives, we must help the needy in very ordinary and practical ways. Every day, individuals walk past those who have no one else to turn to. We can ignore those in need of shelter, food, clothing or whatever it may be. If we look deep in our hearts, this could be because we believe they have brought this condition on themselves, maybe through the result of addictions, unwise choices or even laziness. Though this sounds harsh, it is the viewpoint of many and stops them giving to those in need, even though it may not be the case. The church can be in danger at times of adopting this attitude.

## God's heart for the Poor

In Scripture we see that there are over 300 verses that talk about God's concern and heart for the poor. Looking after those in need is a constant theme throughout the book. An example from the Old Testament is in Deuteronomy 15. God sets out what the Israelites should do for the poor that they came across. If anyone was in need, they were to open their hands to them and freely give. In the New Testament, we see that looking after the poor and the needy was a key activity of the early church. Alongside this, believers shared their possessions with one another and as a result "there was no needy person amongst them" (Acts 4:34). It wasn't just once a year when they reached out or at a special event that was being held; it was part of their daily lives.

## Our Response

We must realise again our individual and corporate role of looking after the poor that are among us. The church in Acts showed us a great example of how to do this. In this day and age, we can feel like we are doing our bit for the poor by throwing some loose change into someone's paper cup. It must become much more than that. Our attitude towards those in desperate situations needs to change from fear and disdain, to love and action. This could be the avenue from which God can come into their lives and transform their circumstances.

God also promises blessing to those that look after the poor. He regularly tells his people that when they engage with the needy, his favour will be upon them and they will be rewarded. "Give generously to them and do so without a grudging heart; then because of this, the LORD your God will bless you in all your work and in everything you put your hand to" (Deuteronomy 15:10). God makes it really clear what the benefits are.

## Our attitude

When we help the poor, our attitude should be right. The following are 3 keys that can help us in our giving:

1. Give with a smile – God loves a cheerful giver. Don't give begrudgingly or reluctantly. It must come from a place of compassion rather than a feeling of being forced.

2. Be extravagant – don't just give a little. It is easy for us to do this because we won't really miss it. Demonstrate the goodness and extravagance of God in your care and giving.

3. For God's eyes only – Jesus commented on the Pharisees and how they announced to everyone that they were giving to the needy. They wanted to be recognised by men for what they were doing. Jesus said only those who do these things in secret will be rewarded.

---

*"We met Barry on a busy city centre street where he took soup and a roll from us, and, as he got to know us a little, he told us his story. He had been working on a building site as a foreman, and as he walked along scaffolding, he fell from about twenty feet, sustaining injuries to his head and back. It turned out he had had an epileptic seizure which was a surprise as he had never taken one before. After examination, he was diagnosed with a tumour behind his retina which was the cause of the seizure causing him to fall at his work. We offered to pray for him, he accepted and he left some time later. We met him again two months later and he was all excited to tell us he had not had a seizure again since the night we prayed for him. He now wants to join us on the streets to help others"* - Phil

---

## Have a Look

Read Jesus sharing the parable of the sheep and the goats in
Matthew 25: 31-40

What did the righteous do?

.......................................................................................................

.......................................................................................................

.......................................................................................................

.......................................................................................................

.......................................................................................................

What was their reward?

.......................................................................................................

.......................................................................................................

.......................................................................................................

Why were their works so important to God?

.......................................................................................................

.......................................................................................................

.......................................................................................................

## Practical Response:

If you see someone begging or living on the streets this week, offer
to buy them a drink and something to eat. It doesn't take that long
to get something. You may pray into their situation with them. It is
only going to be God that really changes their life.

## Questions for Reflection:

1. What do you now understand about God's heart for the poor?

2. Why is it easy to ignore those in need? Why do we do it?

3. Do you see your actions changing towards the poor?

**\*\*\*\*\*\*\*\*\***

**Growth Point:**

Consider financially giving to an organisation that works with the poor in some way. It could be a one-off donation or through regular giving. The charity may be based somewhere in your own town or city, or even working internationally. There are multiple ways to give to the poor such as through sponsoring a child and giving to health and food programmes. We may not be able to reach them but we can enable others to help, as long as we don't use this as an excuse to ignore the needy we see in front of us.

**\*\*\*\*\*\*\*\*\***

# 23. Being the Message

*Advancing the Kingdom*

*"Come with me. I'll make a new kind of fisherman out of you. I'll show how to catch men and women instead of perch and bass"*
*– Jesus*

Evangelism is a word we may hear often in Christian circles. It's a subject that scares most people. It can have many negative connotations that will cause people to shy away from it. The thought of having to convince someone to follow Jesus is petrifying. We get images of performing sales pitches to non-believers to get them to convert, combating all their arguments with well-rehearsed answers. This is the picture some have, alongside standing on a busy street with our soap boxes. No wonder many Christians are frightened to evangelise.

## Evangelism

Evangelism is simply what we do that tells and demonstrates God and his message to those who are not yet believers. It is the invitation we give that allows people to discover there is a God and that he loves them. What we do to make this happen is not limited by techniques or certain methods. There are many different ways we can share the message. Individuals will connect with the story of Jesus through varying means - through conversations, talks, music, videos, creativity ...the list keeps on going! Jesus showed us a great model for being effective in evangelism. We could probably write a separate book on that topic all together. Some of the key things we see from his life about sharing the Kingdom message are the following: he met people where they were at, he challenged, he did it with power and he said that anyone could do it. In church, there are those that are clearly what we call 'evangelists.' However this does not mean that they do all the work in bringing people to Jesus. We all have a role to play in this. The good news that we have is surely too good to keep to ourselves. The message of the gospel that brings new life, hope and restoration is something the world is crying out for. We must let people know through our words but also through the way we live.

## Be the Message

A well-known preacher used to say: "Preach the gospel - and if necessary, use words". One of the most effective ways to spread the good news, rather than just telling our message, is to live our message. Individuals should look at our lives and see the difference God makes. It should make them want to say, "I want what you have". When the world looks at us, they should see the favour of God on our lives and this will open the doors for them coming in (Psalm 69). Below are four keys to being someone who really lives the message:

1. Love - Love God and love others, constantly choosing to prefer others, to forgive and to honour them.
2. Give – Be generous with your time, talents and money. It reveals part of the nature of God.

3. Speak – What comes out of our mouths can bring death or life (Proverbs 18:21). We must watch what we speak out but also we must speak up when the time is right.

4. Act – True faith in God will lead to action. There is some truth in the saying "actions speak louder than words". Your actions show what you truly believe.

## Telling Your Story

One of the key things we can do that will share God's message with others is learning to tell our own story. By doing this, we show how the power of God changes lives today. It is not just something we read about historically, it is something that has impact in the here and now. He is a personal God so let us show people through telling them what he has done for us.

> *"One of the reasons why I started to take notice of Christianity was because of the individuals I knew that followed Jesus. I looked at their lives and realised that they had something I hadn't seen in others before. There was such life, hope and love in their lives. I had heard about God many times previous, however it was only as I began to see that it could make a difference to people's lives that it caused me to be intrigued. These people helped me to understand more about God in a real way and in a way where I could identify with it. It wasn't through a sermon or a pamphlet explaining Christianity; it was through listening to their own personal experiences and it made the whole thing real. Through their actions I could see they really believed in this whole God thing!"*

**Have a Look**

Look up the following verses and write down what you see about God's heart for those that don't know him:

*1 Timothy 2:3-5* ...............................................................................

...............................................................................

...............................................................................

...............................................................................

*2 Peter 3:9* ...............................................................................

...............................................................................

...............................................................................

...............................................................................

*Ezekiel 33:11* ...............................................................................

...............................................................................

...............................................................................

...............................................................................

**Practical Response:**

If you had just one minute to tell someone what God has done in your life, what would you say? What would be the keys things you would include? How would you say it in a way which would be relevant to them? Take some time to write down what you say.

**Questions for Reflection:**

1. What were the key events that helped you come to faith?
2. What are the different ways you have seen Christians tell and demonstrate the good news? Have you seen these make an impact?

3. How do you see yourself growing in each of the areas mentioned in the "Be the Message" section?

**\* \* \* \* \* \* \* \* \* \***

### Growth Point:

Focus on one person you would like to see come to know God. Pray for them daily and ask God for ways you can demonstrate his love to them. Be active in looking for ways so that they may encounter God and give their lives to him.

**\* \* \* \* \* \* \* \* \* \***

# 24. Passing it on

## Advancing the Kingdom

*"Go and make disciples of all nations, baptising them in the name of the Father and of the Son and of the Holy Spirit, and teaching them to obey everything I have commanded you"*
*– Jesus*

We close this section by looking at two very important elements that we must know about for being part of changing people's lives. These are leading someone to faith and how we can help those that do start their journey with God.

## Leading someone to Christ

When we reach into the world, individuals may receive a powerful encounter with God. They can realise his love for them in that moment. As a result, they may be ready to receive Jesus as their Lord and Saviour or it could be a significant step towards this. If the first is true, how do we lead someone to Jesus?

On two separate occasions in Acts people ask the question: "How can I be saved?" In the first instance, Peter responds to the crowd by saying: "Repent and be baptised, every one of you, in the name of Jesus Christ for the forgiveness of your sins. And you will receive the gift of the Holy Spirit" (Acts 2:38). When Paul and Silas are asked, they say: "Believe in the Lord Jesus, and you will be saved" (Acts 16:31). In Scripture, there is no step-by-step way set out of how someone comes to faith in Jesus. However we know it should contain the following key elements:

1. Must believe in Jesus – They must have an understanding of what they are doing and why they are doing it. There should be a realisation of who Jesus is and what he has done for them before accepting him as their Lord and Saviour.

2. Repent – This is more than just saying sorry. It is a full 180 degree turn from sin and embracing a new way of thinking and the new life.

3. Be baptised – This won't happen immediately. However it is a key part in signifying that the old has gone and new life has come.

4. Receive forgiveness – They should embrace the forgiveness given by God. The slate has been wiped clean. They are a saint.

5. Filled with the Holy Spirit – Important for any new believer, receiving the Holy Spirit.

## Be part of discipleship

Jesus told us to make disciples. As part of this, we should help build those up that come into the Kingdom and help them grow and mature in their faith. We see this in the Bible where individuals helped train others to develop even further in the ways of God. Paul with Timothy is an example of this. We should gather around those that come in so that we can aid the process of releasing them into the fullness that God has for them. It may be that we feel we do not have much to give. However, our experiences can really help new believers grow, even if it is just at the start. Simply meeting up for a coffee can allow you to input into their life and it can help them move forward. They may be able to identify with your story, and the same questions you had at the beginning you can help work through with them. People can fall away if they do not have strong foundations in their faith and a benefit of discipleship is it can put this in place. We must look after one another so that we all progress to become more like Jesus.

---

*"Coming from a non-religious background, my first introduction to Christianity was through mentoring. Truthfully the only reason I entered Christian circles initially was because the youth church had a group where I could play the Playstation. However through chatting with the guys who ran it, I got to know them and their faith a lot better. So when times got hard for me and I was finding things difficult, I knew I had somewhere I could turn and people I could talk to. The advice and support I was given during these times showed me for the first time the practicalities and effectiveness of Christianity, and was key in me deciding to start my own journey in discovering God. The relationships I formed back then have stayed strong even to this day and knowing that I had somewhere to turn without fear of being judged or looked down on helped me realise that I would never be too far away from God to come back. Because of the amazing benefits I got from being mentored, I was inspired to start to disciple others myself and being able to help and guide others through difficult times towards their potential and destiny is the most fulfilling and rewarding thing I've done."*- Brian

**Have a Look**

Look up Ephesians 2:8-10.  It relates part of the message we should be sharing with others:

How have we been saved?

..................................................................................................

..................................................................................................

..................................................................................................

Who are we in God?

..................................................................................................

..................................................................................................

..................................................................................................

Why have we been created?

..................................................................................................

..................................................................................................

..................................................................................................

**Practical Response:**

Many Christians have found having someone in their life who they can go to for wisdom and encouragement has contributed a lot to their growth in God. Is there someone with that little bit more experience that could support you in your journey? Someone you could meet up with and be accountable to, and who can pray for and encourage you? Pray and see if God reveals someone to ask. It is a relationship that is more than just seeing one another at church meetings!

**Questions for Reflection:**

1. Do you think you can tell if someone is ready to give their life to Jesus? What do you think are the signs?

2. What is your definition of the term "disciple"?

3. What are the key things you have learnt through this book that you would want to pass on to someone just starting their journey with God?

**\*\*\*\*\*\*\*\*\*\***

### Growth Point:

Always think whether there is anyone you can be investing in. Is there a new believer around that you could help and encourage in some way?

**\*\*\*\*\*\*\*\*\*\***

# What about Baptism?

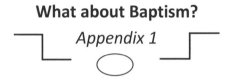

*Appendix 1*

Baptism is a command Jesus gave to his disciples (Matthew 28:19). We shall look at the meaning of baptism and the act of being baptised, but first let's see where the idea came from.

### Where did the idea of baptism come from?
In the Old Testament the people were told to wash when God was going to meet with them in a special way – Exodus 19:9-11. When Jesus was on earth, a Gentile (that is a non-Jewish person) could join the Jewish faith, and baptism in water was used in this process. John the Baptist added a further dimension by baptising Jews. This was as a sign of repentance in anticipation of the coming of the Kingdom of God.  Jesus took baptism a stage further when he commanded his disciples to baptise all future disciples in his name.

### The Practice of Baptism
Different churches today practice baptism in different ways, for example infant baptism and believer's baptism. Some sprinkle with water and others fully immerse the person under the water.

### Have a look
Take a look for yourself at what the New Testament says about Baptism: Matthew 3:13-17; Matthew 28:19; Acts 2:38-41; Romans 6:1-4; 1 Corinthians 12:13; Galatians 3:26-27.

## The Meaning of Baptism

In baptism we are making a public confession of our faith in Jesus Christ as Lord. We are identifying with him and his followers. Baptism portrays a powerful 'picture' of the truth that Jesus has cleansed us from sin. Baptism is also like a funeral service where we bury the 'old self' and rise up as a new person in Christ. Our baptism is a wonderful, unforgettable, unrepeatable and spiritually enriching experience. It is a great opportunity to testify to what Jesus has done for you. It is a powerful demonstration of the unseen work of God's grace.

## Being Baptised

When you are baptised you will be asked questions along these lines:

1. Do you believe that Jesus Christ is the Son of God, who lived on earth, died for your sins and was raised again?
2. Do you promise with God's help to follow Jesus and to serve him and his church?
3. Will you confess your faith? (Jesus is Lord).

If you can sincerely answer 'yes' to questions 1 and 2, and declare Jesus as Lord of your life then there is nothing to stop you being baptised.

# Bible Overview

## Appendix 2

This section will help you grasp more of what is in the Bible. It will be able to give you a picture of what you see throughout each book and how it all fits together.

## Old Testament – 39 Books

| Book: | Themes: | Some Key Individuals: |
|---|---|---|
| Genesis | Creation, Sin, Promises | Adam, Eve, Noah, Abraham, Jacob, Issac, Joseph |
| Genesis records the beginnings – of earth, of humanity, of sin and of God's plan to restore blessing to the world through his people. | | |
| Exodus | Rescue, Guidance, Law | Moses, Miriam, Aaron, Joshua, Pharaoh |
| Exodus means "the way out". This book records the story of Israel being freed from slavery in Egypt and shows their initial steps as a nation. | | |
| Leviticus | Worship, Holiness, Offerings | Moses, Aaron, Nadab, Abihu, Eleazar, Ithamar |
| Leviticus highlights the importance of holiness. For the priests, it was a handbook showing their duties in worship. For the Hebrews, it was a guidebook for holy living. | | |
| Numbers | Rebellion, Faith, Restoration | Moses, Miriam, Aaron, Joshua, Caleb, Balaam, Korah |
| Numbers records the story of Israel in the wilderness, on their journey to reaching the promised land. It shows their successes and failures. Also in this book, it reminds us of God's heart for individuals. | | |

| Deuteronomy | Faithfulness, Love, Laws | Moses, Joshua |
|---|---|---|
| Deuteronomy is Moses' reminder to the people of Israel of what God has done for them. He encourages those to rededicate their lives to him. | | |
| Joshua | Fulfilment, Faith, Leadership, Guidance | Joshua, Rahab, Achan, Phinehas, Eleazar |
| Joshua shows the fulfilment of God's promises to Abraham. It shows the journey of the Israelites occupying the promised land. | | |
| Judges | Oppression, Heroes, Repentance | Deborah, Gideon, Abimelech, Jephthah, Samson, Delilah |
| Judges records Israel continually falling into sin and suffering the consequences from it. The "Judges" were spiritual leaders who rescued the people out of these times, after people cried out for God's help. | | |
| Ruth | Faithfulness, Integrity, Blessing, Love | Ruth, Naomi, Boaz |
| Ruth tells the story of how three individuals remained faithful to God and strong in character when others in society were not. | | |
| 1 Samuel | Leadership, Obeying, Faithfulness | Samuel, Saul, David, Jonathan, Eli, Hannah |
| 1 Samuel contains the events of the life of Samuel, Israel's last judge. It shows the preparation of David in becoming Israel's greatest King. | | |
| 2 Samuel | Influence, Justice, Sin, Restoration | David, Solomon, Bathsheba, Nathan |
| In 2 Samuel, David becomes King over Israel. The book highlights David's successes but also the struggles he encountered during his reign. | | |
| 1 Kings | Kings, Prophets, Sin, Repentance | David, Solomon, Rehoboam, Jeroboam, Elijah |
| 1 Kings records the life events of David's son, King Solomon. It also highlights the spiritual condition of Israel and how this impacted them. | | |

| 2 Kings | Idolatry, Judgement, Patience | Elijah, Elisha, Isaiah, Naaman, Joash, Nebuchadnezzar |
|---|---|---|
| 2 Kings shows spiritual leaders who did not learn from the past. They did not make God their true leader. There are a few examples however of those that turn to God and receive the blessings that come with this. | | |
| 1 Chronicles | History, Worship, Covenant | David, Solomon |
| Chronicles is written about the same historical period found in Kings. 1 Chronicles reminds us of Israel's identity through genealogies and also outlines David's preparations for the temple and for the rule of Solomon. | | |
| 2 Chronicles | Prayer, Peace, Reform, Temple | Solomon, Rehoboam,Hezekiah, Josiah, Queen of Sheba |
| 2 Chronicles records the reign of King Solomon and the building of the Temple. It also highlights the events of the Kingdom of Judah, the revolts, reforms and exiles. | | |
| Ezra | Faithfulness, Promise, Rededication | Zerubbabel, Haggai, Zechariah, Ezra |
| Ezra tells the story of God bringing many of the Israelites back to Jerusalem after being in exile in Babylon. It shows God's faithfulness and that he is one who keeps to his promises. | | |
| Nehemiah | Vision, Leadership, Prayer, Rebuilding | Nehemiah, Tobiah, Ezra, Sanballat |
| Nehemiah is the final historical book in the Old Testament. It describes the story of the walls being rebuilt in Jerusalem and the history of the third return for the Israelites after captivity. | | |
| Esther | Deliverance, Wisdom, Change | Esther, Haman, Mordecai |
| Esther illustrates how someone with great courage & wisdom can impact many. Through prayer and with God, great things happened in her reign. | | |

| Job | Suffering, Faith, Trust, Goodness | Job, Eliphaz, Bildad, Zophar, Elihu |
|---|---|---|
| This book records the life of Job. Despite losing everything he had including his wealth, family and health, he learned that when nothing else was left, He had God and that was enough. | | |
| Psalms | Praise, Thankfulness, Worship, Forgiveness | David, Asaph |
| The Psalms are a collection of poems, songs and prayers showing praise, worship and confession to God. Mainly written by David, you will discover in them a whole range of human experiences. | | |
| Proverbs | Wisdom, Speech, Success | Solomon |
| The book of Proverbs holds keys in how we attain wisdom and discipline in our lives. It's a collection of wise sayings showing us how to life godly and fruitful lives. | | |
| Ecclesiastes | Emptiness, Work, Wisdom, Searching | Solomon |
| Ecclesiastes shows us that life is meaningless without God. The book shows us lessons from Solomon's life in how our own knowledge, popularity, wealth and pleasure will not give us purpose or meaning. | | |
| Song of Songs | Sex, Love, Beauty, Commitment | Solomon, The Shulammite Woman |
| Song of Songs tells of a love between a bridegroom and his bride. It's a story about married love and also a picture of God's love for his people. | | |
| Isaiah | Holiness, Messiah, Salvation, Prophecy | Isaiah |
| Isaiah means "Salvation of the Lord". Isaiah is the first of the major prophets. This book calls the nation of Judah back to God and prophesies God's salvation through the coming Messiah. | | |

| Jeremiah | Sin, Faithfulness, Messiah | Jeremiah, Ebed-Melech, King Nebuchadnezzar |
|---|---|---|

In this book, Jeremiah confronts many people with their sins. He encourages the nation to turn back from God. Jeremiah brought a hard message but something that people needed to hear.

| Lamentations | Mercy, Sin, Hope, Warnings | Jeremiah, People of Jerusalem |
|---|---|---|

Lamentations contains Jeremiah's mourning and weeping for a destroyed Jerusalem. It highlights again that there are consequences to sin, however also that in the midst of troubles, there is hope.

| Ezekiel | Holiness, Sin, Restoration, Worship | Ezekiel, Nebuchadnezzer |
|---|---|---|

The prophet Ezekiel's book announces judgement on Israel and other nations. However in this there are messages of future restoration and hope to the people, showing that God will never abandon his people.

| Daniel | Faithfulness, Purpose Perseverance | Daniel, Shadrach, Meshach, Abednego, Nebuchadnezzer |
|---|---|---|

The book of Daniel highlights that no matter what is going on, God is in control. This book records an account of faithful Jews who lived in captivity and gives a preview of God's future redemption.

| Hosea | Sin, Love, Restoration, Judgement | Hosea, Gomer |
|---|---|---|

Hosea is the beginning of the minor prophets. This book demonstrates God's love for a sinful people, despite their unfaithfulness.

| Joel | Holy Spirit, Forgiveness, Sin | Joel, People of Judah |
|---|---|---|

Similar to other Old Testament books, Joel warns the people of the time of the consequences of sin and urges them to turn to God. Joel also prophesies of the day when God's Holy Spirit will be poured out on all.

| Amos | False Religion, False Comforts, Justice | Amos, Amaziah, Jeroboam II |
|---|---|---|

The prophet Amos delivers prophetic messages to Israel regarding their sinfulness. He reminded them that true faith comes from the heart, rather than just what they say.

| Obadiah | Self-sufficiency, Justice | Obadiah, The Edomites |
|---|---|---|

Obadiah means the "servant of the Lord". His book shows what happened to the nation of Edom as it stood and watched God's people and land being invaded.

| Jonah | Compassion, Repentance, Mission | Jonah |
|---|---|---|

God sent Jonah with a message to Nineveh to turn from their wicked ways and turn to God. The book of Jonah records the story and shows that God's grace and his salvation is for all people.

| Micah | Faith, Oppression, Repentance | Micah, People of Jerusalem and Samaria |
|---|---|---|

The book of Micah emphasises the need for peace and justice. It warns God's people again that sin must be punished however there is grace for those that repent.

| Nahum | Rulership, Judgement | Nahum, People of Nineveh and Judah. |
|---|---|---|

Nahum shows that despite how great a nation or empire is, they must still give an account of their actions to God. The book of Nahum shows that God that can be overcome by no one.

| Habakkuk | Struggle, Hope, Sovereignty | Habbakkuk, The Babylonians |
|---|---|---|

Habbakkuk records the doubt that this prophet had in what God was doing. Through the answers he sees, he responds with a prayer of faith.

| Zephaniah | Wrath, Hope, Self-sufficiency | Zephaniah, People of Judah |
|---|---|---|
| Zephaniah's message came to shake the people of Judah out of their complacency and to tell them again to come back to God. Zephaniah speaks of a day of wrath but also that a day of hope will come. | | |
| Haggai | Encouragement, Temple, Priorities | Haggai, Joshua, Zerubbabel |
| Haggai is a call to the people to complete the rebuilding of the temple in Jerusalem. Individuals had focused on other priorities; Haggai encouraged the people to focus again on the temple. | | |
| Zechariah | Purity, Temple, Protection, Messiah | Zechariah, Joshua |
| The book of Zechariah was an encouragement to the people of God who were in exile. Through visions and words of encouragement, Zechariah showed the people of God what blessing was on its way. | | |
| Malachi | Love, Sin, Messiah | The Priests, Malachi |
| Malachi encouraged those who were disheartened through telling of God's love again. However in this, he called the people to restore their relationship with God from where it had fallen away. | | |

## New Testament – 27 Books

| Book: | Themes: | Some Key Individuals: |
|---|---|---|
| Matthew | Messiah, Kingdom of Heaven, Teachings | Jesus, Mary, Joseph, Disciples, Pilate, John the Baptist |
| Matthew is the first of the gospels that shows the life, death and resurrection of Jesus Christ. It was written specifically for the Jews to show that Jesus was the Messiah that had been prophesied. | | |
| Mark | Miracles, Teachings, Mission | Jesus, Disciples, Pilate, Religious Leaders |
| Mark is the shortest of the gospels. It presents the person, work and teachings of Jesus and emphasises his servanthood. | | |
| Luke | History, Holy Spirit, Compassion, Saviour | Jesus, Elizabeth, Zechariah, Mary, John the Baptist, Herod |
| Luke is the only known Gentile author in the New Testament. The purpose of his gospel is to record an accurate account of Jesus' life and to show that Jesus was the perfect human and is our saviour. | | |
| John | Salvation, Life, Holy Spirit, Son of God | Jesus, John the Baptist, Mary Magdalene, Lazarus, Martha |
| John is the last of the gospels. It inspires faith and shows that true salvation can be found through Jesus. It records Jesus' most memorable saying, his longest sermons and most profound miracles. | | |
| Acts | Church, Mission, Holy Spirit, Courage | Paul, Peter, John, Stephen, Luke, Barnabas, Silas, Philip |
| Acts records the events of the birthing and the exponential growth of the early church. It focuses largely on the ministry of Peter and Paul who through the Holy Spirit perform many miracles and preach boldly. | | |
| Romans | Salvation, Sin, Growth, Gospel | Paul, Phoebe and the people of Rome |

| | | |
|---|---|---|
| This is Paul's letter to the people of Rome outlining the good news story and how it applies to their lives. It provides good foundations for believers. | | |
| 1 Corinthians | Gifts, Worship, Sin, Freedom | Paul, Timothy |
| 1 Corinthians is a letter to the Church in Corinth in which Paul addresses the problems and the questions that the Church was facing. It gives wisdom on how to sort division and disorder alongside instructions regarding marriage, personal freedom and public worship. | | |
| 2 Corinthians | Doctrine, Trials, Hope, Discipline | Paul, Timothy, Titus |
| Paul's second letter to the Church in Corinth is written to defend attacks on his character and authority. Paul talks about his message, ministry, and character. He also calls the Church not to be taken in by false teachers. | | |
| Galatians | Salvation, Freedom, Law, Faith | Peter, Paul, Barnabas, Titus |
| Galatians is a call to Christians to a life of faith and freedom. It challenges the viewpoint that many had at that time that salvation can be achieved through obeying the law rather than solely through Jesus Christ. | | |
| Ephesians | Encouragement, Church, Family | Paul, Tychicus |
| The letter of Ephesians summarises the message of grace. It was written to strengthen believers in Ephesus in their faith and shows how to live by Christ's new standards | | |
| Philippians | Joy, Unity, Humility, Sacrifice | Paul, Timothy |
| Philippians is Paul's letter that encourages believers that true joy can come no matter what circumstances are happening around about them. | | |

| Colossians | Holiness, Freedom, Christ | Paul, Timothy, Mark, Tychicus, Onesimus |
|---|---|---|
| Colossians confronted some of the false teaching that was appearing in the Church at Colosse. In this letter, Paul reminds us of what Christ has done for us and how this brings freedom in our lives. | | |
| 1 & 2 Thessalonians | Persecution, Christ's Return, Faithfulness, Persistence. | Paul, Timothy, Silas |
| Paul's 1st letter to the Thessalonians strengthened the young believers there. He praised them for their faithfulness and encouraged them to continue to please God in their daily lives. Paul also highlights the importance of Christ's return and what that should do for us. His 2$^{nd}$ letter continues this theme and corrects some misunderstandings. | | |
| 1 Timothy | Leadership, Discipline, Church | Paul, Timothy |
| Paul's first letter to Timothy gave wisdom to this young leader on how to keep God's household in order alongside how to continue to live a life devoted to God. | | |
| 2 Timothy | Courage, Suffering, Faithfulness | Paul, Timothy, Luke, Mark |
| This letter is sometimes seen to be Paul's "famous last words". He encourages Timothy to stay strong in his faith and even when the difficult times come to remain faithful to God. | | |
| Titus | Relationships, Church, Character | Paul, Titus |
| Titus had the responsibility of supervising churches on the island of Crete. Paul's letter encourages him and us today to continue to live devoted to God even when society is not. He reminds us that our faith should lead us into action. | | |

| Philemon | Forgiveness, Love, Respect | Paul, Onesimus, Philemon |
|---|---|---|
| This letter reminds us that our attitudes and relationships are transformed in Christ. We are to see people through eyes of love and despite what they have done to us, we must express God's love to them. | | |
| Hebrews | Maturity, Faith, Endurance, Christ | Jesus, Abraham, Moses, Melchizedek |
| Hebrews highlights the superiority of Christ. We see that the new covenant brought by Jesus, supersedes what has been before. The writer encourages us to press in for genuine faith rather than legalism. | | |
| James | Faith, Love, Kingdom of God, Action | James |
| The book of James gives us a simple "how-to" guide on being a Christian. It covers various themes showing us that our faith must not only be in talk but also in action. | | |
| 1 Peter | Persecution, Faithfulness, Family | Peter, Silas, Mark |
| Peter's first letter offers encouragement to those Christians that were suffering and going through many "fiery" trials. In the early church, persecution was arising; Peter wrote this to strengthen their faith. | | |
| 2 Peter | Truth, Growth, Maturity | Peter, Paul |
| As Christians, we should continue to mature in our faith. Peter warns us against false teachers and tells us we should hold onto the truth. | | |
| 1 John | Love, Life, Light | John, Jesus |
| The first of John's letters is written to reassure Christians in their faith. It highlights the importance of showing God's love to one another. | | |
| 2 John | Truth, Love, Teaching | John, Chosen Lady, Children |

| 2 John is a short letter that commands us again to love one another. It also reiterates that we should not let false teaching impact us or others. | | |
|---|---|---|
| 3 John | Faithfulness, Hospitality, Care | John, Gaius, Demetrius, Diotrephes |
| In this letter John encouraged those who were kind to others and taking care of Christian workers. It reminds us to support one another and continue to show generosity. We should avoid just looking after ourselves and pursuing our own agendas. | | |
| Jude | Truth, Faith, Perseverance | Jude, James, Jesus |
| Similar to other previous letters in the New Testament, Jude's has the focus of warning believers against false teaching and to remind Christians to stay strong in their faith. | | |
| Revelation | Hope, Judgement, Christ's Return | John, Jesus |
| Revelation is the final book in the New Testament. Through a vision John received the book reveals what will happen in the last days. It shows us that there will come a day when evil and injustice will not prevail and gives us great hope that with Christ's truth, victory is assured. | | |

# Christianese Dictionary

## Appendix 3

In Church, there are many words that are used that can be seen as "Christian jargon". There are terms that we can hear that we may be unfamiliar with and will seem alien to us. Below is a short dictionary of some of those, so that we can know what they really mean and realise the fullness of the term. We must remember that in speaking with others we need to keep it simple so that people can understand us and we ensure that we know what we are talking about!

| Word: | Meaning |
|---|---|
| Apostolic | Relating to apostles who pioneer new works of the Kingdom of God. |
| Communion | Also called 'Eucharist' or 'Lord's Supper' this refers to the meal that is observed in remembering Jesus' death. |
| Consecrated | Set apart for a special purpose of God. |
| Discernment | Wisdom to know what is of God and what is not. |
| Evangelism | The communicating and demonstrating of the good news about Jesus. |
| Fellowship | Really means a shared life with a common purpose, but is often used to describe believers meeting together. |
| Glory | This refers to the weight or worthiness given to God, or the revelation of his nature and power. |
| Holy | That which is set apart from the ordinary as belonging to God. |

| | |
|---|---|
| Humility | A true appreciation of ourselves from God's perspective. |
| Justification | The concept of having been justified and found not guilty in God's sight by Jesus' saving act on the cross. |
| Missionary | A person sent to a place or people group to make Jesus known there. |
| Prophecy | A communication (word or act) that reveals something from God into a present situation. This may include a sense of what is to come or simply be a word of encouragement. |
| Redemption | The concept that Jesus has paid the price to buy us back from the enslaving power of sin. |
| Repentance | The act of turning to God and changing the way we think. |
| Righteous | Having a right standing (right relationship) with God. |
| Salvation | The concept of being rescued from sin, sickness and evil, and brought into wholeness in Jesus Christ. |
| Testimony | A witness's account of what God has done for them. |
| Witness | To witness is used to mean to tell someone about your faith in Jesus. |

"I have come that they may have life, and have it to the full" – John 10:10

If you would like additional resources or other information regarding the book, look up our website at www.lifetothefull.info

*Contact the Authors:*
Write to:
Healing Rooms Scotland
PO Box 7010,
Glasgow
G76 7UL
U.K.

Email: steven@healingrooms-scotland.com or james@healingrooms-scotland.com